SMALL-BUSINESS MANAGEMENT GUIDE

ALSO BY JIM SCHELL

The Brass-Tacks Entrepreneur

SMALL-BUSINESS MANAGEMENT GUIDE

Advice from
the Brass-Tacks Entrepreneur

JIM SCHELL

Henry Holt and Company
New York

Henry Holt and Company, Inc.
Publishers since 1866
115 West 18th Street
New York, New York 10011

Henry Holt® is a registered trademark of Henry Holt and Company, Inc.

Published in Canada by Fitzhenry & Whiteside Ltd.,
195 Allstate Parkway, Markham, Ontario L3R 4T8.

Library of Congress Cataloging-in-Publication Data
Schell, Jim.
Small-business management guide: advice from the brass-tacks entrepreneur/
Jim Schell.—1st ed.
p.   cm.
Includes index.
1. Small business—Management.   2. New business enterprises—Management.
3. Small business—Personnel management.   4. Success in business.   I. Title.
HD62.7.S33   1994
658.02′2—dc20   94-4598
                                                                      CIP

ISBN 0-8050-3399-8

Henry Holt books are available for special promotions and premiums.
For details contact: Director, Special Markets.

First Edition—1994

Designed by Katy Riegel

Printed in the United States of America
All first editions are printed on acid-free paper. ∞

10   9   8   7   6   5   4   3   2   1

To Mary, my wife and friend,
and to Jim, Todd, and Mike,
without whom I'd be much richer.
And much poorer.

Contents

Acknowledgments

*Thanks to
Lynn Odland,
Gary Adams,
Randy Duncan,
Frank and Amy Johnson,
Tom Moe,
and Tom Rootness.*

Foreword

What's a nice person like you doing in a "situation" like this?

Let me guess.

If you're like me, you've decided to entrepreneur your life away because the alternative—collecting a paycheck—has proved to be hazardous to your health. Too constrictive, perhaps, or too much like home or school or juvenile detention center. Stifling and un-creative.

So, what happened?

So you started your own business and that business grew, and the more it grew the more employees you hired, and the more employees you hired the more structure you required. And soon you had this throng of people milling aimlessly around your desk. People needing direction, people needing motivation, people needing their problems resolved. And lo and behold, before you could scream "don't fence me in," you were up to your ears in the same misery you originally set out to avoid.

People. They either make us or they break us; there's no middle ground. And (spare me a dissertation on today's social ills) there are plenty of good people around. And if they don't perform the way we would like them to, it isn't their fault. After all, we hired them. And should have trained them. And should have motivated them. And yes, we could have fired them if that's what was needed.

Let's face it, people aren't furniture or fixtures or pieces of equipment. They are sensitive, and moody, and unpredictable. They require a framework in which to prosper and that framework is called management, and management can be oh so restrictive.

I'm sorry to inform you that I don't have a magic formula for washing management out of your hair. There is no such thing as "management-free," where small business is concerned anyway. Someone has to lead, someone has to hire, fire, and promote, and someone has to sign the bank's guarantee.

And that someone is the entrepreneur, in the early stages of the business at least. The entrepreneur: a free spirit who would much rather be moving and shaking and trying something new than managing people. A free spirit who chose this unstructured profession because he never liked the confinements of structure in the first place.

All right, so maybe we can't avoid management, but we can learn how to mold it. Mold it to suit our personal needs, our company's needs, and the needs of our employees.

This book is about employees and entrepreneurs, and the molding and entwining of them into and around the framework of management. It's about making the process work for everyone.

Let's face it—management is no easy task, especially for those of us with management-unfriendly traits. But easy or not, we had better start managing people the same day we hire our first employee—which coincides with the same day we'd better start focusing, and delegating, and following up, and communicating, and listening, and making people accountable for their actions, and on and on into the world of things that managers must do.

And that entrepreneurs don't know how to do. Or don't want to do. Or weren't meant to do.

But assuming we're committed to the growth of our business, which means a life of dealing with people, there's a way to ease the pain. A way to graft the structure of management to the creativity of the entrepreneur. A way to create the best of all possible worlds.

The answer is a combination of corporate management techniques and entrepreneurial flexibility.

First we take those management techniques, systems, and rules that our corporate brethren have developed over the years and toss them with a generous portion of flexibility. Flexibility in dealing with employees, flexibility in leadership techniques, and flexibility in vision. Then add a dash of inventiveness and a pinch of creativity.

And Eureka! What do we have? A flexible manager who can still answer to the word "entrepreneur."

In Part I, I discuss the entrepreneur's role in the growth of his business, as well as the number one reason for failure. Part II defines the term "flexible management," and then it's on to building the team (Part III), organizing the team (Part IV), and motivating the team (Part V). From there I move into culture creating (Part VI), the making of a flexible manager (Part VII), and getting the most out of the entrepreneur (Part VIII). Winding down, we look at the entrepreneur's role and the choices he must make (Part IX) before closing with a collection of tips to grow by (Part X).

At this point, a discussion of gender is in order. I've referred almost exclusively to "he" and "his" throughout this book. I could just as well have used "she" and "hers," but opted for the ease of tradition. I beg the indulgence of my female readers.

For those of you who read my earlier book, *The Brass-Tacks Entrepreneur*, you will find similarities between that book and this one. These similarities are deliberate and necessary.

The Brass-Tacks Entrepreneur provided its readers with an overview of the entrepreneuring profession, from the inception of a business through its sale. The *Small-Business Management Guide* is a more tightly focused book that concentrates on the "people" aspect of building a business. Primary emphasis is on assembling, motivating, and managing a team, along with making the transition from entrepreneur to manager.

I'm convinced there is nothing new in this world. Everything that can happen has happened, except maybe where Louisiana politics is concerned. And most of those things have happened to me, when it comes to people and problems and the growth of a small business, anyway.

And I've learned over the years that there are only two kinds of people in this world—those who cause problems and those who don't. I've never met one of those who don't, nor has one ever worked for me. Maybe they've all worked for you, in which case you've just wasted a few dollars on this book.

But if you have some of these problem-causing employees buried in your payroll someplace, you're sure to discover them in the upcoming pages. Along with suggestions on how to solve their problems.

Yes, I did say, "solve their problems." After all, isn't that what management is all about?

I

It's Capital. No, It's the Niche. No, It's the Entrepreneur!

1

The Entrepreneur
as the Wizard
of Oz

Remember the Wizard of Oz? The eccentric old fellow at the end of the yellow brick road, the one with the frizzy hair? The guy who sat behind the curtains, pulling his levers, pushing his buttons, growling at the rest of the world?

Well, everything that ever happened in his castle happened because of him. And so it is with us entrepreneurs. Inside our small-business castle we're wizards, too, just like the Wizard of Oz. Whatever happens in our company happens because of us. We control the levers we pull, the buttons we push, the words we growl. We call the shots.

But just because we call the shots doesn't mean we have all the answers. (The Wizard of Oz certainly didn't.) Or do all the work. Or deserve all the credit.

But it does mean we have the means to direct those who do the work. And those who deserve the credit. After all, they are our employees and we hired them. And should have trained them, and compensated them, and motivated them. Yes, and could have fired them, too, if the situation had warranted it.

And if all that power isn't enough, we also created the very environment that our employees thrive in. Or don't thrive in. For the horse comes first in the culture-setting business: we create the culture and *then* our employees proceed to succeed. Or proceed to fail if we've hired the wrong employees and created the wrong culture.

Which reminds me of Mr. W. Edwards Deming.

Mr. Deming, a world-renowned management theorist, was the principal reason that Japan became the global symbol of industrial reliability in the post–World War II era. The Japanese listened to Deming when the United States wouldn't. In later years Japan's success finally opened the United States' eyes, and Deming became one of the principal architects of our late eighties and early nineties resurgence in manufacturing. He was truly a man committed to his message, a bona fide international hero, until his death at age ninety-three.

Deming subscribed to one overriding principle in his quest to help the industrial world improve its lot. That principle was that it is management that wins or loses the industrial game. Manufacturing output and quality are not a function of labor's whims, but rather of the breadth of management's leadership. Led properly, Deming preached, workers produce. Led shoddily, they don't.

And so it is with our small business. If our company wins, we are responsible. And if our company loses (and 60 percent do), we are also responsible. It isn't the fault of our employees (we hired them), and it isn't our systems (we hired the employees who built them), and it isn't our customers (we hired the employees who found them). Nor can we blame our failures on our niche, because we picked it in the first place.

No siree. It's 100 percent us.

That's why we're like the Wizard of Oz.

And that's where this book begins. It begins at the beginning. With us, the entrepreneur, perched in our castle, manipulating the controls. And if we want our company to grow, our management skills had better grow, too.

Growth, the path to small-business success. No one survives without it. Everyone prospers with it.

THE BOTTOM LINE

The entrepreneur wins or loses as a result of the people he hires and the culture he creates.

The entrepreneur controls his own destiny. He pulls the ultimate levers. He calls the ultimate shots.

2

The Number
One Killer

All right, it's time for a test. Books closed. Ready? Here's the first question:

"What's the number one cause of small-business failure?"

All hands shoot up.

"What's that? No, it isn't undercapitalization. Or lousy location. Not poor distribution, either. Give up?"

All heads nod.

"The answer is loneliness. Entrepreneurial loneliness."

All right now, admit it. You were wrong, too.

Undercapitalization and bad location and poor distribution aren't causes of failure, they're only symptoms. Symptoms of that dreaded disease, Entrepreneurial Loneliness. Unnecessary symptoms that wouldn't have to occur if we availed ourselves of guidance and help.

What happens is that the same crusty independence that sucked us into this career in the first place now stands in the way of our success. We learn our everyday lessons by the process of trial and error, repeating the same tired, energy-draining mistakes our predecessors have been making for so many years before.

How wasteful it is to go it alone, instead of taking advantage of someone else's experiences. And how sad. And expensive. And yes, so often fatal. We stumble along, day after bone-tired day, week after seventy-hour week, never seeming to get ahead, and can never figure out why. If we can only get through this week, this month, this year, we keep telling ourselves, our problems will finally disappear. Our business will get off its tired duff.

So what happens? We get through this week, this month, this year, and guess what? We've got an entirely new set of problems, and our duff's more tired than it ever was before. And still we don't catch up.

Sound familiar?

Seeing as how I'm a charter member of the never-bring-up-a-problem-without-a-solution club, I have an antidote to this Entrepreneurial-Loneliness disease. Or several antidotes, if you prefer. Use one or use them all.

I. Find a Partner

Small-business studies show that partnerships outperform sole proprietorships by wide margins. Or, to resort to the trite, two heads are better than one.

And two heads are dramatically better than one when the second head contains skills the first one doesn't. If entrepreneur number one is a sales and marketing type, number two should be a financial type. Or an operations type. Or an administrative type.

OK, so I know partners can be, and often are, a pain in the neck. Or in other anatomical zones. But everything has its price.

In this case, the trade-off has statistically proved to be worth the risk.

2. Find a Mentor

An entrepreneur, current or past. Preferably a grizzled one. Some-one who's been there before. Someone who knows what it's like to meet a payroll, to feel the hot breath of unhappy bankers, to know what it feels like to pink-slip a friend or, God forbid, a relative. Someone who has experienced the experience.

That someone is out there somewhere. Network to find him. Inquire of accountants, lawyers, bankers, vendors, and friends.

Leave no stone unturned in the search. Mentors can save time, money, and headaches. Sometimes the business. Oftentimes the career.

3. Use a Board of Directors

Not only a board of directors, a board of directors composed of outsiders. No insiders please—we must stamp out rubber stamps on the board. (And if a board of directors doesn't work, try a board of advisers.)

Listening and following up does not have to be hazardous to the entrepreneur's health. Besides, a little accountability never hurt anybody.

4. Network

It won't be long before every city in the United States has its own entrepreneurial networking organization. A sort of matchmaking service, one that gets entrepreneurs together, mixes them, matches them, and spoon-feeds them information and resources based on the experience of others.

If your city doesn't have such a network, it should have. It's a viable niche and one that needs filling. For profit or for fun. (This niche is currently being filled in my hometown. For profit, too.)

So what's holding you back? Start a network of your own. What kind of an entrepreneur are you, anyway?

5. Read

Peruse the shelves of your nearest library or bookstore. You won't believe the number of books written on the subject of small business. Ex-entrepreneurs, academics, accountants, consultants—you name it and someone has written about it.

And magazines, too. *Inc.* and *Entrepreneur* and all applicable trade magazines should be required reading for every entrepreneur. There are others, as well.

6. Join

Small-business associations are everywhere, offering advice along with a number of networking advantages. Local and national, public and private, these associations come in all sizes, shapes, and forms. Consult your local library's business reference section for an up-to-date list of resources.

And don't forget trade associations. Every industry has at least one.

7. Take Advantage Of

U.S. government offerings. After all, you pay for them. Contact the Small Business Administration. Also your local Small Business Development Center. Most major cities have one.

Dun and Bradstreet also offers a variety of services to the small-business person. Call them.

And don't forget your local college and university business

schools. Most want to help, and even those that don't can direct you to places that will.

As a fellow named Henry Wheeler Shaw once wrote, "Solitude. It's a good place to visit, but a poor place to stay." He was talking to us.

THE BOTTOM LINE

Experience is the best teacher. Go find some.

If the entrepreneur spent one-tenth the energy in seeking guidance and assistance that he does in seeking capital and customers, he'd save ten times the effort in unmade mistakes.

3

Managers Aren't Mushrooms

And now, a word about *managers*. A dirty word to many of us, but a word we had better understand. Because the day we hire our first employee is the day we begin to be one.

Managers aren't mushrooms. We can't pot them in a dark basement and watch them grow overnight. Making the transition from entrepreneur to manager is a process, not an event—a long and painful transition that begins that same day we hire our first employee and ends when we hire our last. Or fire our last.

And managers don't grow forever. As Akers and Sculley discovered in 1993 (John Akers, ex-CEO of IBM, and John Sculley, ex-CEO of Apple Computer), everyone maxes out sooner or later. We all reach our managerial peak.

So how will we know when we've reached ours?

When our balance sheet begins to sag. When our profit-and-loss shudders and coughs, when cash tightens, and when our stress level rises at the same pace as our credit lines. When last year's seventy-hour weeks shrink to forty. When Saturday mornings are for golf and pruning the roses, and work isn't fun anymore.

And it won't be our industry that's at the root of our problems. Or our employees, or our products, or a spate of bad luck. Sure, all of the above will be symptoms, but the real illness will be us.

Quite simply, our manager fuel will have run out.

Exactly when will our gauge plunge to empty? That depends on the strength of our niche (a good niche can hide a wealth of mistakes), and the quality of the employees we've hired. Oh yes, and on how many of a long list of managerial shortcomings are ours.

But most important, the timing of our descent into manager's hell depends on how committed we are to making the transition from entrepreneur to manager, how dedicated we are to upgrading our managerial skills and overriding our entrepreneurial shortcomings.

Me? My manager fuel ran out at $25 million in sales, but I could have made it to $50 million had I recognized my shortcomings earlier and done something about them. Who knows, with a little luck and a lot better hiring, maybe I could have hung around long enough to make it to $100 million.

You? Who knows, maybe you're a Bill Gates or Sam Walton. Talented, focused, and in the right niche. Maybe you can take your company to $1 billion in sales. Maybe $50 billion.

But sooner or later the Peter Principle of Management goes to work on us all. It's inevitable, like the rising cost of health care and the shrinking value of inventory.

But it doesn't have to be sooner. It can be later, if we begin planning today.

So take a chance, before it's too late. Make the commitment to improve your management skills. To learn and to change. But don't expect to make that transition too quickly.

Mushrooms may sprout overnight, but good managers need plenty of time.

THE BOTTOM LINE

Everyone has managerial limitations. But self-awareness, when combined with a willingness to change and a manageable ego, can extend those limitations far beyond their natural boundaries.

II

The Keys
to Flexible
Management

4

Everything Else
Is a Guideline

Management systems are like legal systems. Neither is really a system, even though that's what we call them. They're more like a framework.

Take our legal framework, for instance. We've been fiddling with it for centuries, but there just aren't enough rules and regulations to cover all the strange things people do. Thus we can never leave our legal framework alone. We're forever tweaking it—daily, monthly, yearly—straining to stretch it and bend it and make it function as we want it to. But still it doesn't work smoothly. Never will.

Why? Because of us, the very people our legal framework is intended to govern. And protect. The same people that foul it up in the first place. People. Scheming, conniving, complicated people.

And those same scheming, conniving, complicated people are busy fouling up our management systems, too, and the underlying reasons are the same. That's because both these systems are frameworks, and there are two ways that people fit into frameworks—hardly, and not at all. People have too many options. They zig when they ought to zag. There has never been a framework invented, nor will there ever be, that can encompass the wide range of people's moods, emotions, and idiosyncrasies.

Like the government that spawned our legal framework, it is only as good as the people who oversee it. And the roster of these overseers starts with the cop on the beat and ends with the Supreme Court.

Well, ditto with management. Except that the small-business process begins with the line supervisor and ends with us, the entrepreneur, our company's Supreme Court. And if we oversee our management framework judiciously, then it will function as intended. If we don't, it won't.

All of which means that the best management system isn't the one with the most rules. Or the tightest framework. Or the trendiest name. It means that the best management system is the one with the best manager overseeing it.

Consider an organization chart for a moment. The key to an efficient organization chart isn't the manner in which it's constructed. The key is how it's used. If we decide to pigeonhole our employees inside those little rectangular boxes, then we won't have an organization chart anymore, we'll have a repression chart. Or a depression chart. Or a regression chart. An organization chart must be flexible (meaning, among other things, that dotted lines are OK), similar to the people it is intended to organize.

We must realize when applying that organization chart that people aren't employees first and foremost. They are Homo sapiens, with all of Homo sapiens's warts and blemishes. They are kings and queens, bishops and rooks, knights and pawns, and there is an infinite number of moves we can make with them, many of which circumvent the rules and regulations of cut-and-dried management. And our business wins or loses as a result of the way we manipulate, and sometimes circumvent, those cut-and-dried rules and regulations.

That is to say our business wins or loses by the way we flexibly manage our people.

And so you see, it all comes down to this. The key to successful management is the manager himself. That's us.

And the key to our success is flexibility.

If managers are flexible, systems won't be systems anymore, they'll really be guidelines. That means if we've promised to ship a customer's order tomorrow, and the order-entry system won't allow it to ship until next Wednesday, then we circumvent the order-entry system. And by God, we ship it tomorrow. System or no system. (An act that makes order-entry clerks wince, but puts broad smiles on the faces of customers.)

If we're flexible, rules and regulations aren't rules and regulations anymore, they're really guidelines. If our rules call for two weeks of vacation, and one of our employees has a family emergency, then it's three weeks of vacation without batting an eyelash, and we'll work out the details later. Rule or no rule.

If we're flexible, strategies aren't strategies anymore, they're really guidelines. If today's strategy calls for X, and opportunity Y suddenly appears, then it's heigh-ho, heigh-ho, and off to Y we go. Strategy or no strategy.

I'm not saying there aren't some rules and regulations that must be inviolate. We do need hard and fast directives to manage our computer system, for instance, as well as real estate, and inventory, and any other asset that doesn't have a central nervous system.

But add a central nervous system and all bets are off. People are imperfect, whether they're managers or managees, and we've got to make provisions for those imperfections. And the provisions we make come from flexibility, and that flexibility comes from us.

OK, so you're thinking of a successful business somewhere that makes me a liar. A Schwarzkopf & Sons perhaps, where spit and polish, rules and regulations, yes-sirs and no-sirs, are the order of the day. The left foot goes in front of the right, straight lines prevail, and damn the torpedoes, full speed ahead.

But the problem with spit and polish organizations is that the kinds of employees they require are hard to find these days. People have changed in the last fifty years and most of today's workforce won't swallow that hardball management style anymore. (Sure, I know it's your company and you can do what you want. And if you don't mind spending half of your waking hours looking for employees to fit Schwarzkopf & Sons' mold, then go for it. But don't say I didn't warn you.)

And don't give me the song and dance that business is war and needs to be run like the marine corps. After all, even the marines acknowledge there are only "a few good men" who can swallow the structure the marine corps demands (and entrepreneurs aren't typically among them). Besides, if you are in a business where one mistake makes the difference between life and death, then go read Schwarzkopf's book. You're wasting your time reading mine.

In today's business environment, there isn't much that's inflexible. Everything from missions to goals, from visions to strategies, from industry trends to government policies, is in a constant state of change.

Fortunately, change is an integral part of our entrepreneurial birthright.

Let's hope it stays that way.

THE BOTTOM LINE

Where people are concerned, frameworks and charts and rules and regulations aren't systems, they are only guidelines.

The only thing flexible enough to manage people is people.

5

What's Flexible.
What's Not.

I've got this problem with buzzwords. They're too transitory, too spur-of-the-moment, gone faster than a crooked bookkeeper with yesterday's deposits. As a result I've tried to avoid them. I must admit, however, where the term "flexible management" is concerned, I've come dangerously close.

I'm sorry, but I can't help it. The definition of flexible management is "proven management techniques bent and twisted," and it fits our proactive, growth-friendly, entrepreneurial businesses to a T. But, as you may have noticed, I didn't title this book *Flexible Management Techniques*. Nor do I claim ownership of the term, and I'm not nominating it for the Buzzword Hall of Fame.

And I'm not saying that everything we're responsible for should be flexibly managed, either. To the contrary, we need a sprinkling of inflexible rules and rigid regulations included among our management tools. We need them to help us manage our:

- Ethics and principles. If ethics and principles aren't inflexible and inviolate, they aren't ethics and principles.
- Fixed assets. Anything that doesn't go home at night. Real estate, equipment, furniture, and fixtures.

- Expense controls. The eighties are gone. Finished. Kaput. The best companies today are those that are as aware of their expenses as they are of their sales. Expenses need to be controlled with rules, regulations, and, yes, an iron fist.
- Quality. There can be no flexibility where quality is concerned. The product is either fit for the most demanding customer or it's unfit. There is no middle ground.
- Working hours. A business where employees are allowed to drift in (and out) is either enjoying the greatest niche in the world or approaching Chapter 11. Drifting in and out might work for those businesses with only a few employees, but put a dozen or so drifters on a payroll, and listen for the whir of the turnstiles.
- Substance abuse. No flexibility here. Not in my company, anyway.

But where people are part of the entrepreneurial environment, flexible management is the order of the day. Everything, from the customers we covet to the visions we create, needs to be managed flexibly. For instance:

- Employees. There are two kinds of employees in this world, those who care and those who don't. I'll break most rules for employees who care.
- Customers. There are also two kinds of customers, those who view us as partners and those who view us as patsies. I'll break almost every rule for a partner.
- Mistakes. Mistakes are OK. Oh, I don't love them and I don't encourage them, but if they're only made once, and made for the right reasons, they're an integral part of the learning process. But don't make the same mistake twice.
- Visions, missions, goals, strategies, and plans. Damn right they change. There are too many variables.
- Organization charts. For administrative purposes only.
- Performance reviews. Necessary, but no forms, please.

One employee's motivator can be another employee's depressant.

- Committees and consensus. Most of the time they're the right thing to do, but occasionally they're not. Sometimes they take too much time, and sometimes the issue doesn't warrant the effort. And remember, that's your name you've signed on the guarantee.

This book is primarily about people. But not about just any old people, mind you. We're talking about the most complex, frustrating, and potentially rewarding people in the world.

We're talking about employees, and if you don't value yours above every other asset in your company, then I've got a suggestion for you. Pass this book on to someone who does.

THE BOTTOM LINE

Employees are people and no two are the same. They are our most important asset and must be managed flexibly.

Real estate is real estate and equipment is equipment. Real estate and equipment are not our most important assets and can be managed inflexibly.

6

W. C. Fields
and Customer Service

It's fashionable these days to subscribe to the business dogma that says, "Customers are everything." After all, customers buy our products, pay our bills, and give us an excuse to play golf on Wednesday afternoons. We should live and die for our customers, we are led to believe.

Well, with all due respect to the "customers are everything" proponents, I disagree. Customers aren't everything. Employees are everything.

I don't give a damn how good our customers are, if W. C. Fields is taking our customer-service calls, our customers won't be customers very long. The same thing applies if Jack the Ripper is making our sales calls. Or if Rodney Dangerfield is handling our public relations.

See what I mean? Ineffective employees equals disappearing customers. Every time.

We are told how to treat our customers. How we should listen to them. Communicate with them. Protect them. Coddle them. Handle them like visiting royalty.

I don't disagree.

But shouldn't we deal with our employees the same way? Even

more so? After all, somebody has to design the product that our customers buy. And somebody has to produce it. And sell it. And ship it. And bill it.

No employees, no customers. (Or: Wrong employees, no customers.)

All of which means that our number one job (and nothing is even close to second) is to assemble a team of the finest employees a small business can muster.

How? By making a crusade out of hiring. By turning it into a science. By gritting our teeth, setting aside whatever else we're doing, and never resting until we've hired a team of the finest employees in the land.

And then proceed to train the hell out of those employees. At the same time we are motivating them, and compensating them, and treating them like—like customers. And yes, now and then we've got to swallow hard and fire an employee, before he drags down the team.

And if we do our job right, we'll have a team on our payroll, and teams get things done. And if we don't do our job right, we'll have a collection of individuals on our payroll, and individuals cause problems. And don't get things done.

The single most important lesson we must learn as entrepreneurs, CEOs, or flexible managers is the value of our employees. It is we who should be thankful to have them on our payroll, not vice versa. And until such time as we acknowledge their role in our life, and until we make them number one on our priority list, and until we treat them as well as or better than we treat our customers, our company is doomed to mediocrity. Or worse.

THE BOTTOM LINE

The company with the best employees gets the best customers. It's never the other way around.

And the company with the best customers always wins.

23

III

Assembling and Building the Team

7

Yea, Rah, Rah, Team

There are six million entrepreneurial businesses in the United States with one or more employees. Of those six million, only 7 percent, or 420,000, boast more than $500,000 a year in sales.

Does that mean that those 420,000 businesses have the best products? The most cash? The best locations?

Maybe. Maybe not.

But this much I can tell you for sure. Each of those 420,000 businesses is headed by a leader (or two, or three) who understands the value of leverage. And furthermore, that leader understands that leverage comes through a collection of people who constitute teams—and the leader who assembles the best team always wins. In sports and in politics and in business.

And not only do these 420,000 leaders understand the value of leverage, they also have done something about it.

Yea, rah, rah, team.

Now don't get me wrong. Individuals have their role in the growth of a business, too. The start-up that roars out of the block in its incubation years is usually headed by the most energetic, most hell-bent-for-leather, most do-it-yourself achiever in town. You

27

know who I mean, the swashbuckler willing to risk it all, the entrepreneur leaving the biggest cloud of dust in his or her wake. Mr. or Ms. Full Speedahead. But lifting a start-up off the ground is one thing, keeping it off the ground is another.

And propelling it into the rarefied air of those 420,000 businesses is yet quite another.

The start-up that reaches that rarefied air will be the one that's led by the entrepreneur who has assembled the best team. The team that together can do the things the entrepreneur is unable to do. Or at least the things he doesn't have time to do because he's too busy performing his team-building duties.

And speaking of teams, as already mentioned, partnerships outperform sole proprietorships, where the growth of small business is concerned anyway. Not just by the hair of your chinny-chin-chin either. Paul Reynolds of the Center for the Study of Entrepreneurship at Marquette University found that only 6 percent of the fast-track small businesses he traced were founded by one person—54 percent had two founders, 40 percent had three or more. Meanwhile a startling 42 percent of the slow-growth start-ups he discovered traced their heritage back to one founder.

Strike a statistical blow for the benefits of a team. No, make that a knockout punch.

Obviously insiders, that is, partners and employees, are the number one components of a team, but there can be outside elements as well. Boards of directors, or advisory boards, can be major contributors to teams. Along with mentors, shareholders, and yes, even bankers. (If I were my banker and had as much cash tied up in my company as he did, I'd want to be a part of my team, too.)

It's so obvious. Why don't we independent-to-a-fault entrepreneurs understand it? Business isn't golf, it's football. The best team always wins, not the best individual.

A team, by my definition, anyway, is a collection of people with a similar purpose and goals. And those collections come in a variety of forms. We small-business owners, in our environment, have the sole power to determine that form.

Our entire company can be one team, for instance, especially in those early start-up days. Later on, teams might be organized according to function—departments, or day shifts, or night shifts. We can form teams to advise and recommend—ad hoc committees and project teams and brainstorming teams. Teams can be permanent or teams can be temporary. Teams can be managed from the top down (the traditional team), bottom up (the solve-an-operational-problem team), or not at all (the self-managing team).

Do your team organizing whichever way works best. Creativity is always acceptable where teams are concerned.

And finally I must warn you, teams aren't airplanes and they won't fly on automatic pilot. There has to be a team-friendly culture for a team to prosper, the establishment of which is the sole responsibility of the entrepreneur. (More on the subject of culture later on).

All right, I can hear you saying, enough is enough. I understand the importance of teams. So how do I begin to assemble mine? Where do I start?

I thought you'd never ask.

THE BOTTOM LINE

Labels and nicknames don't make teams. People make teams. And structures and guidelines don't foster teams. Cultures foster teams.

The entrepreneur hires his employees and establishes the culture. The entrepreneur creates his team.

Like people, teams must be accountable for their actions. As well as their inaction.

8

Our Number One
Responsibility

We've determined (I hope we have, anyway) that our most important asset is our employees. OK, if we're agreed that this is the case, then our number one chore in creating a successful business is to make sure that our number one asset is managed by a team of superstars in key leadership positions. Or, stated another way:

The small-business owner's number one responsibility is to assemble a team of superstars in game-breaker positions.

Once these people are secured in those game-breaking positions, we can delegate whatever our number two responsibility is.

What are those game-breaking positions? That depends on the company. Most often there will be four or five, starting at the top with us (the president or CEO), and including the financial person, the sales manager, the marketing manager, the operations manager, the office manager, and the purchasing director. (Admittedly, few small businesses have all these positions filled, but regardless of title, whoever it is that performs the above-mentioned duties should be of superstar status.)

What is a superstar? Every entrepreneur is allowed his own definition and the criteria may vary. To me, a superstar is someone who:

1. Is capable of more than presently assigned,
2. Is loyal to the entrepreneur's vision and mission,
3. Shares the entrepreneur's ethics and principles,
4. Speaks his mind,
5. Is creative within his area of expertise,
6. Adds to the synergy of the team,
7. Welcomes change.

That's my definition anyway. What's yours?

Why don't we hire superstars for every position? Just think, an entire company bulging with superstars. How sweet it would be. Our managerial life would be simplified, our business survival guaranteed.

Wonderful in theory. Certainly worth striving for. But impossible to achieve.

That's because superstars don't become superstars overnight. They don't show up on our doorsteps clutching their diplomas. Superstars require time—time to develop, time to mature, time to learn. And most of all, time to train, training that generally must come from the outside. From those who train better than we do. (Usually our Fortune 500 cousins.)

Which is not to say we shouldn't strive to hire superstars in their pre–Fortune 500, budding stages. We too can set our standards high and look for the same employees that Xerox and IBM strive to find. But don't expect those employees to become the superstars we seek unless we're prepared to train them. And to supervise them. And yes, to pay them. Superstars, budding or otherwise, respond to supply and demand. They don't come cheap.

Nor will today's superstars remain superstars forever. Jobs change. Responsibilities change. People change. A superstar at $5 million in sales can be a superdud at $10 million. Some people keep up with change, some don't.

And that new hire we thought was a budding superstar? There can be many reasons why he won't be. Maybe our hiring was flawed. Maybe the office synergy isn't right. Maybe the job isn't what he thought it would be.

So what does all this mean? It means that the search for superstars is an ongoing process. A never-ending quest. A quest for perfection that, like all quests for perfection, will forever elude us. (But the entrepreneur who comes the closest will win.)

And finally it means that we have to learn how to manage employees who are something less than superstars. Because we'll always have some of them working for us, in one stage or another. And because our superstars will have some of them working for them, too.

Now try this. Take an inventory of your employees currently filling game-breaking positions. How many are superstars, by your definition?

Next, a more difficult question. What do you intend to do about those employees in game-breaking positions who don't measure up to your definition of superstar status? Do you intend to:

1. Do nothing? (Always the easiest route.)
2. Immediately terminate those who come up short?
3. Determine how many have the potential to become superstars, then train them and motivate them, and if, after all that, they still don't make the grade, replace them? (The most difficult route and one we'll discuss in subsequent chapters.)

What happens when we select the first of the three options? Mediocrity, at best.

The second? Automatic failure. (Even legitimate superstars will hit the road once we start firing old-line employees without first giving them the opportunity to improve.)

The third? Superstars for our team. Fat city for us.

Here are a handful of tips on how to accumulate and develop that team of superstars:

1. The best indicator of how any employee, superstar or otherwise, will perform in the future is how he's performed in the past. Trust yesterday's actions and not today's words when interviewing outside candidates or promoting from within.

2. Of all the attributes to look for in assembling superstars, responsiveness to change is the most important. Resistance to change by a key member of the management team is the surest way to impede future growth and destroy opportunity.

3. There must be a degree of compatibility among the team members. They must agree on the company's destination and goals, and must individually subscribe to the value of a cohesive team. They need not, however, agree on the best course to pursue in reaching that destination.

4. When hiring superstars, remember you are not hiring individual performers, you are hiring team players—individuals with a proven ability to perform in a team environment. Superstars must be able to work in a crowd and leverage themselves, for that is the key to personal business growth.

5. A company enjoying slow growth can, given the wide window of time it is allowed, usually find and develop superstars from within. Rapid growth almost always requires hiring from the outside, something most entrepreneurs are reluctant to do in the face of loyalty to longtime employees.

6. Treat superstars better than customers. Do whatever you can do to solve their problems, then sit back and watch the good times roll.

And don't spend one-tenth of a second telling me that the reason our team of superstars isn't performing is the poor quality of its members. That's a cop-out. There are plenty of good people out there; it's our job to find them. And hire them. And keep them.

Make no mistake about it, the problem when the team isn't performing is us. We've either hired the wrong superstars, or we're leading the right ones in the wrong direction.

THE BOTTOM LINE

Not to be forgotten in the quest for superstars: The leader of a team of superstars must be a superstar himself. If he isn't, his choices are two. Upgrade himself or move on.

Over prolonged periods of time, the team with the most superstars wins.

9

Don't Settle
for Less
Than the Best

In his book *No Excuses Management*, author and entrepreneur T. J. Rodgers outlines his version of kamikaze hiring. Rodgers, a successful Silicon Valley CEO, relates how he targets a competitor's employees, forms a posse of his finest executives (he calls them "raiding parties"), and flies into Dodge City, literally infiltrating the enemy's camp, laying siege to it. Once there, his raiding party hunkers down in Motel Command Central and doesn't budge until its hiring mission is completed. Until Mr. Wonderful is safely ensconced in Rodgers's land of milk and honey.

Now I'm not saying that all of us should take hiring to this extreme. But Rodgers has built a successful company in a killer industry (semiconductors) by making damn sure his team has more superstars than his competitors. So far he's been right.

Rodgers knows you don't build crackerjack teams without hiring crackerjack employees (he personally signed off on *every* employee until his company reached a thousand employees). Hiring is obviously the number one chore on his to-do list, and when he goes on a hiring binge, nothing gets in his way. (Why should it, when he has so many good employees to delegate the rest of his duties to?)

All of which leads me to the number one rule of the number one way in which we perform our number one chore:

The best employees go to the entrepreneur who is willing to go to the most trouble to find them.

Hiring's no art, it's a science. And a much less exciting science than, say, oceanography or archaeology. It's methodical and it's repetitive and it's a drawn-out, ho-hum, brain-numbing process that consists of one aggravating detail after another.

Success at the science of hiring requires rigid attention to detail and focus on the issue at hand, those proven and reliable entrepreneurial killers. If we are going to hire right, we must interview, and reinterview, and reinterview again. We must pick up the phone and check those always-exciting personal references, whose primary function in life, we soon learn, is to tell us as little as possible between rushes of glowing adjectives. We must ask the right questions, listen between the lines, and leave no lapses in time unquestioned. We must jump on the most obscure danger signals and pursue them with vigor until they are revealed as either the darkest of secrets or the deadest of ends. We must focus on the issue at hand and beat that torrent of details to death, all the time wishing we were doing something else—making a sales call, perhaps, or walking the manufacturing floor.

Try the following exercise the next time a superstar hire is necessary and you aren't psyched up for the task: try attaching a dollar cost to your failure.

Assume, for instance, that you have a $10 million, rapidly growing company and are shopping for a superstar CFO. What will it cost if you hire the wrong person? The cost can be computed by adding the expense of the mistakes that are sure to follow, plus wasted training time, plus the expense of rehiring and starting all over again.

The answer, in the above example, anyway, is a minimum of a half-million dollars, a maximum of Chapter 7, and untold years of regret. I should know, it happened to me in a somewhat different form. The cost was somewhere in between, and I'll pay until the day I die. And I have no one to blame but myself. I did the hiring.

The process of hiring a superstar should proceed something like this:

Interview 1: Takes place in your office amid a barrage of questions with the interviewee doing 90 percent of the talking. (If he doesn't do 90 percent, you're talking too much.) Immediately following the interview, begin the reference-check process, while the details are still fresh in your mind.

Interview 2: On neutral turf this time, maybe for breakfast or lunch. Relax him, loosen him up, get a look at his social and personal side. Ask those puzzling questions that have emerged as a result of the reference checks.

Interview 3: If all has gone well, have the applicant go through the interviewing process with several key employees who also have a stake in the success of the hire. Ask their opinions. Compare. Discuss. Listen. After all, if he isn't going to mesh with the team, it's better to find out sooner than later.

Interview 4: Review, negotiate, and close, if he still passes muster. And then cross your fingers. There are no guarantees in the science of hiring no matter how thoroughly a job is done. The odds will improve with experience, but failure is always lurking nearby.

Here is a list of hiring hints to help locate that elusive superstar:

1. The best candidates come from inside-the-company references. Establish a system to encourage your employees to introduce qualified candidates. Include rewards.

2. There's no substitute for a professionally organized interviewing process. After all, what candidate with superstar creden-

tials would consider employment with a company that can't interview professionally? Orchestrate your interviews, and prepare for them meticulously. Make them mirror what superstars seek.

3. The hiring process requires you to wear two hats. The first is the hat of the detective, as you attempt to determine whether the applicant is a hero or a bum. The second is the salesman's hat, to be donned once the hero is found. Don't forget to prepare for the second role, and don't incorrectly assume your company is the only, or the best, opportunity in town.

4. The best hires are usually the ones that are the most difficult to close. Negotiations are bound to be tense and the process drawn out. The procedure can be exhausting, often to the point of evoking anger, but isn't this the kind of negotiator you eventually want on your side?

The better the applicant, the more difficult he will be to sign. Winners have more options than losers. Or, stated another way, beware of the hire who signs too easily.

5. Try to establish some ground of commonality between the reference checks and yourself, thereby opening the door to more candid conversations. Most references talk warily, having read horror stories of the legal liability inherent in passing public judgment on others. Look for the little things as you listen, and read between the spoken lines. Ask about the applicant's weaknesses, then multiply by a factor of five.

Bad references are as rare as an honest politician. That's because most references double as the candidate's friends.

6. The best references are those the applicant doesn't list. Review the resumé, then network friends and business acquaintances to find third-party references who will talk out of school.

7. Look for the applicant's ability to listen as well as to speak. If he doesn't listen during an interview, he sure won't listen on the job.

8. Probe carefully for cultural mismatches during the questioning process. Some things will never change in people, no matter how diverse your company's culture.

9. By dissecting the motives behind the applicant's questions (and he had better ask some good ones), you can learn what it is that is important to him. What does he want to know about you? Are his questions meaningful? Sensible? Logical? Is he looking for a place to hang his hat, or does he want to make a contribution?

10. What research has the applicant done on you? If he comes to the interview unprepared, you are learning something about either his work habits or the depth of his desire for the job.

11. Favorite interviewing questions of mine:

- What are your weaknesses?
- What are your strengths?
- Why should I hire you?
- What differentiates you?
- What do you want to be doing five years from now?
- What is your most significant business achievement?
- What is your biggest failure and what did you learn from it?
- What would you like to know about me and about my company?

12. While on the subject of questions you should ask, there are a number of questions you can't. You can't ask the applicant's age, race, religion, citizenship, or political persuasion. And you can't inquire about parental status, or health.

13. Keep the pipeline of potential superstars full. Maintain a black book of candidates' names, even if you're not currently

shopping. The list should include people who are employed elsewhere but could be lured away from their current jobs. Let your employees know of the black book, so they can help keep it filled.

14. The good applicants will want to know exactly what the job entails, and what is expected of them. Prepare a professionally written job proposal before making your offer, a proposal that delineates everything the applicant might want to know. Include job definition, salary, bonus, perks, time frames, and your expectations.

15. Beware of those applicants who are hung up on the issue of security. They should be employed by the government or a bank, not an entrepreneurial business that depends on the vagaries of the marketplace for its survival. And beware of applicants with 4.0 grade point averages. They see too many reasons why not to.

Instead, hire the glint in the interviewee's eye.

There's an endless list of benefits that come from hiring right. The biggest? The better the employee, the less time will have to be spent managing him. Instead we can spend our time in front of the customer, or on the production floor, or working with product development. Doing those things we enjoy the most (and do the best), while leaving the rest to our team of superstars.

Effective hiring, unlike understanding cash flow or filing corporate tax returns, does not require a rocket-scientist IQ. There are endless books on the subject, as well as seminars, classes, and consultants ready to help locate and hire the superstar of our dreams.

With all this assistance at our fingertips, there's no excuse for failure.

Our only enemy is ourselves.

THE BOTTOM LINE

Hiring is an acquired skill. The more experience, the better the results.

Never delegate the hiring of superstars, and sign off on every hire.

Every position has a related cost of failure, with the CFO at the top of the list and the sales manager not far behind.

Hiring the best employees makes the entrepreneur's life easier. The best ones don't require motivating or baby-sitting; they only need training and liberating.

10

Filling In
the Voids

As I said earlier, cash is not the number one cause of small-business failure. Neither is niche, location, or a competitor's vengeance.

The number one cause of failure is loneliness. The entrepreneur's loneliness. Remember?

So why is it this loneliness of ours is so costly?

Two reasons. First, because we waste our precious resources making the same stupid mistakes our predecessors have been making for years. Unnecessary mistakes, avoidable mistakes, mistakes that can add up and sink our small business faster than a California savings and loan.

Mistakes that would never have been made if the right person had been around to advise us, if the right information had been available to us, and if we had chosen to take that advice and heed that information.

Second, because we have too many make-it-or-break-it bases that aren't being covered because our time is being spent doing something else. Those empty bases that result from our choosing to spend our finite time doing the things we like to do, leaving those we don't like to fall through the managerial cracks.

You know the uncovered bases I'm talking about—the jobs we don't like, the boring jobs, the jobs that require skills we don't have. Bases that would be covered if the right person were around to cover them.

Which means that as our company grows we must be sure to hire the right employees to fill in the voids. Employees who will make it their responsibility to:

- Clean up the mess. Attend to the forgotten details. Pick up after the entrepreneur. (If that someone isn't around, those messes are bound to accumulate and fester. And often prove fatal.)
- This someone can be anyone. Sometimes it will be the financial person, sometimes the office manager, sometimes the secretary. And yes, sometimes the spouse.
- Be the devil's advocate. Question the entrepreneur's sacred intuition, asking the "what ifs" instead of the "when tos." Someone to balance the boss's eternal optimism.
- Get the product out the door. Ship it and bill it and deposit the proceeds.
- Collect the receivables. Every successful company has someone dedicated to collecting the monies due it. If this person isn't the entrepreneur, it had better be someone nearby.
- Make the internal systems flow. Shuffle the paper, program the computers, dot the i's and cross the t's.
- Become a sounding board for the rank-and-file employees. Give the entrepreneur feedback from those nooks and crannies he doesn't have the time or the energy to visit.
- Handle all of those personnel/human relations/government issues that drive most entrepreneurs nuts. Which include just about every personnel/human relations/government issue I can think of, from worker's comp to exit interviews to employee handbooks.
- Give the entrepreneur a view from the outside. An unbiased and impartial view. And yes, a frank and refreshing view, a view that only outsiders can provide. (Most often this view is provided by mentors or an outside board of directors.)

Maybe, in the early stages of our business growth, we can find the time to assume one or two of these specialized duties ourselves, like getting the product out the door or making the systems work. But the more our company grows, the thinner we're bound to be spread, no matter how many hours a week we work, no matter the commitment we're willing to make.

Contrary to our way of thinking, we can't do everything ourselves. But we'd better make sure everything gets done. It won't get done by itself.

THE BOTTOM LINE

Leave no responsibility unassigned. All details need tending, all jobs need doing, no matter how insignificant, no matter how small.

Fifty-million-dollar companies can afford the luxury of hiring someone to fill every void. Two-million-dollar companies can't.

IV

Organizing and Appraising the Team

11

It's the One
with the Boss
on Top

I don't like organization charts. Never did. But neither could I avoid them.

But wouldn't it be a relief if we could? We'd just wave a magic wand and *poof,* the job would get done, by the best person available to do it. How sweet it would be—no politics, no layers, no passing the buck.

That won't happen, of course, not in my lifetime, anyway. You can bet your company's future on it. The organization chart, in one form or another, is here to stay.

Sure, I know there are folks who turn their organization charts upside down. And there are probably horizontal charts, too, and oval charts and isosceles charts. Maybe even trapezoid charts. But for 99 percent of the small-business world, it's the traditional chart that gets the job done.

Remember? The one with the boss on the top.

That's not to say, however, that the boss must be on the top of every decision. Not this boss, anyway. But I can tell you this, if the decision involves my guarantee to the bank, I intend to sign off on it. And if the decision affects my company's culture, I intend to sign off on it. And if the decision has a major impact on my cash flow, I intend to sign off on it.

No upside-downs for me when the future of my company is at stake. That's what I'm paid for.

Of course I'll listen, and if I've collected the right team, that's all I'll have to do most of the time, other than nodding my head in agreement and smiling a lot. I don't need the power that comes from being on top. But sometimes I do need the hammer.

Yes sir, the traditional organization chart always worked for me. I needed its chain of command. Somebody must manage each one of my employees, and pay them, and judge their performance. And promote them, and demote them, and yes, sometimes replace them. Somebody has got to work for somebody. And answer to somebody. And be accountable to somebody, like it or not.

I'm the first to admit that not much is sacred in the business of doing business, including organization charts. Maybe fifty years from now the chart we're using today will be history, too, as management (which will still be around in one form or another) becomes more creative and more trustworthy. Which is fine with me, because the message inherent in organization charts doesn't wear well with me either. But until that time comes, we've got to make do with the tools we've been provided. In the manner in which they're intended.

But organization charts don't have to be inviolate. We should feel free to use them flexibly, to circumvent their layers and tiers to accomplish our projects, resolve our problems, and take advantage of our opportunities. We should feel free to invent a new chart, just for those one-time-only jobs.

A simple organizational circle will suffice for these—nothing more than a circle of involved employees organized around a common purpose: the accomplishment of that project, the solution to that problem, the seizing of that opportunity. Forget the overriding organization chart. Just gather the involved employees, insert the senior stakeholder in the middle, and *whammo,* you have instant empowerment. The organization chart du jour.

Call it a Quality Circle if you will, or a Project Team, or a group of Empowered Employees. Call it whatever is required to make the troops feel warm and fuzzy.

Then stay out of the way and let the folks in the circle get the job done. And if that circle of employees doesn't work, then either you've hired the wrong employees or you haven't trained them properly.

Oh yes, and one more thing. When the project is finished, so is the circle.

Here are several tips on how to best utilize that old standby, the right-side-up organization chart:

1. Don't live or die by an organization chart. Use it administratively, but bend it and mold it to fit the skills of your employees. Flexibility got you where you are today. Don't throw it away on an inflexible organization chart.

2. Don't let the organization chart override the team. Feel free to put junior members in charge of projects when they happen to be senior stakeholders.

3. The organization chart should be built for employees, not vice versa. If one person is particularly strong, give him responsibility outside his designated geography.

4. Don't pay by the organization chart, pay by the quality of the work and the contribution to the team. (I know, I know, this is easier said than done, especially for those musty companies with years of tradition buried in their pay scales. But tradition doesn't last forever, nor does it drop to the bottom line.)

5. How many employees can one person supervise? That depends on who those employees are. One is plenty if that one is like

some I've hired over the years. Fifteen would be a snap if those fifteen were my best. It depends on the people you've hired.

6. Flatter (fewer tiers) is better, when the employees are right. But flatter is impossible when they aren't.

7. Think twice about the employee who insists on a title.

8. And finally, the number one enemy of an efficient organization chart is weak management.

THE BOTTOM LINE

Organization charts are to businesses what prisons are to society. Confining, clumsy, and ever so necessary.

Don't let the organization chart chafe, bind, and restrict. Send your best employee where he can do the most good.

12

Great Expectations

Ten years ago this chapter would have been entitled "Job Descriptions." No longer. In these liberated days, the term "job description" is to small business what sportsmanship is to professional tennis: history. A remembrance of the past.

Today the correct term is "performance expectations."

Sure, a performance expectation is a not too distant relative of a job description, except that it's intended to expand the job, not contract it. It's intended to free employees to bring creativity to their jobs, not restrict them to working within defined parameters. Let's face it, yesterday's job descriptions were always too limiting, too confining, too black-and-white. Too inflexible.

No longer can entrepreneurial companies and their entrepreneurial employees function in a job-description-induced, inflexible environment. In an environment where restriction means contraction and where confinement results in suffocation. Today's employees need space. Elbow room. Room to expand. A well-designed performance expectation provides all three.

Agreed? Then Performance Expectations it is.

Every now and then I read of a liberated soul somewhere whose company survives, and perhaps even prospers, without utilizing performance expectations. (Or job descriptions, or anything else that smacks of structure.) That liberated soul has to be, I keep reminding myself, surrounded by a collection of similarly liberated souls. How else could his company perform?

Well, more power to him and his team liberation if they can grow and prosper without the help of such tools as performance expectations. The more freedom the better, most of us would agree. But that kind of loosey-goosey direction won't work for the majority of us. Most people need a modicum of structure in their lives. The performance expectation provides just that—a loose but reliable framework designed to kick off a four-stage employee appraisal system. Without the support of the performance expectation's framework, the three stages that follow would be doomed to fall flat on their motivational faces.

Here are the four stages of that employee appraisal process:

Stage 1: Performance Expectations. Defines the parameters of the position along with management's expectations. Provides the framework for the following three stages.

Stage 2: Goal Setting. Agrees on the output of performance. (See chapter 13.)

Stage 3: Ongoing Feedback. The process of providing day-to-day managerial assistance. Includes intermittent changes in performance expectations and goals, where required.

Stage 4: Performance Review. The official review of the preceding year's employee appraisal process. And the official beginning of the current year's process. (See chapter 14.)

Each one of these four stages is necessary to the overall success of managing employees. Like baseball and beer, one thrives on the other.

Writing a performance expectation is not a herculean task. It is a one-time job, interspersed with intermittent revisions. (Jobs do change, just as the people performing them change.)

Or, more specifically, expectations do change. For a performance expectation is not intended to focus on the activity of the position, but rather on the anticipated results. Not on definitions, but on consequences. Not on restrictions, but on expectations.

Here is a handful of tips on how to best utilize today's new and improved version of performance expectations:

1. Include a "why" at the beginning of every performance expectation. A brief explanation of the position's objective and how it relates to the overall corporate mission.

2. A brief description of the position's geography: Who is to be supervised, an overview of the position's responsibilities, and a definition of the reporting requirements.

3. Include a position mission statement. The employee should write it himself, subject to approval. When employees change, new position mission statements should be written. They may be the same as the predecessor's, or they may be different. Missions can be in the eye of the beholder.

4. Define the evaluation process—how and when the employee will be appraised.

5. Concentrate on output, not on activity: don't limit the ways in which the job can be accomplished. Define the responsibilities and allow the employee the freedom to make it work.

6. The world changes. So do expectations. Be flexible.

7. OK, so I agree that every position should have a title. Go ahead, give it one. But beware of those who are hung up on the subject.

The biggest mistake we can make is to develop performance expectations that are too restrictive. Today's employees are not yesterday's robots. Nor will they be tomorrow's wallflowers.

Employees no longer long for freedom and flexibility. They demand it.

THE BOTTOM LINE

Focus on results, not on activities.

Remember, you got into this line of work to get away from a stifling job. Don't create another one.

13

A Nod of the Head, a Set of the Mouth

I have three sons, each a joy to his parents, each an asset on the ledger of life. And I wouldn't trade the three of them for three continents, except that when they were in their teens I would have traded them for three cold beers.

They're grown now. You know that's happened when the Father's Day phone calls no longer come collect. And each of the three has embarked on his own missions in life.

The missions of Mike, my youngest, are for his understanding alone, and are as steadfast as his unquenchable wanderlust. They are to (1) ski till he drops, (2) mountain-bike till he stops, and (3) never pass a stream without dropping a fly in it. Or at least soaking a toe. He lives and breathes these unwritten missions, and his quest to pursue them is only occasionally interrupted by his need for sustenance.

More power to Mike, I say, and if I were his boss-between-quests I'd come to understand his personal missions before the two of us determined his on-the-job goals. For nothing but disappointment—on both sides—comes when a business goal interferes with a personal mission.

As surely as corporate goals flow from corporate missions, so personal goals emerge from personal missions. And, in most cases, the employee's personal missions come first, whether we em- ployers like it or not. If our employee's mission is to get involved in politics, or own his own business someday, or make more money than Michael Milken, then we'd best consider his personal mission before establishing his business goals.

Once we've plugged our employee's personal mission into his on-the-job goals, the next step is to make his goals SMART. Here's how the SMART acronym works:

S = Specific: Goals must be clear, direct, and definable.

M = Measurable and meaningful: Goals must be measurable, in the sense that employer and employee can assess whether or not the goal is achieved. And, of course, they must be meaningful to both parties.

A = Appropriate: Goals should be appropriate to the em- ployee's age, experience, training, potential, and respon- sibilities.

R = Realistic: Goals should challenge but be achievable. Eighty percent of the goal should be obvious, 20 percent a stretch.

T = Time limit: The goals should be achievable within the framework of the performance review (usually one year) and always established with an eye toward creating a sense of urgency in the employee's work habits.

I once set goals with one of my CFOs. The goals we agreed upon were SMART and primarily tied to numbers, as CFO goals tend to be. This guy was a bulldog and, it turned out, he achieved his SMART goals with ease, allowing plenty of room to spare.

But his employees and I paid the price. While he achieved his expense reduction goals and his inventory turn goals and his receivable collection goals, he did it through intimidation and stress. His intimidation, our stress.

The message here? Don't forget to define the "how" of the goal achievement process as well as the "what." The end does not always justify the means.

Several tips on the process of goal setting:

1. Remember that goal setting can do much more than foster motivation. It can also help prioritize, at the same time that it bonds setter and settee in a mutually agreed-upon direction. And it allows the goal setter to measure progress in areas where, without the establishment of finite goals, progress would be difficult to measure.

2. Goal setting and planning are first cousins. Plan the route to be traveled before determining the stops along the way.

3. Don't wait until year's end to review progress. Do it informally, when the mood strikes, as well as formally, at quarterly or semiannual intervals.

4. Flexibility is a part of our entrepreneurial charm, as well as our birthright. It's OK if we change goals in the middle of the stream, if the reasons are right. Random events are as dependable as they are unpredictable. Leave room for the unexpected.

5. Unlike entrepreneurs, not everyone derives satisfaction from within; thus goal achievement needs a reward system.

Don't waste any time in making a public announcement once goals have been achieved. Let the celebration begin, and let it be spontaneous and let it be loud.

And remember, there are other meaningful rewards besides financial ones. Fame is meaningful, too, and a lot less expensive than cash. Feel free to mix the two.

6. It's OK for the employee to come up short on his goals. But we should know why, and take steps to see it doesn't happen again.

And finally, goal setting is a communal, bottom-up process. The more involved the employee is in establishing his goals, the more committed he'll be to achieving them. Ask for his tentative goals in advance of the annual review process. Then review them together, hone them together, and write them down. That way there'll be no misunderstanding when it comes time to tally the score.

Then demand the employee's commitment. For if goals aren't subscribed to, the process is useless. And I don't mean acknowledged, I mean *subscribed* to.

Don't mistake the two. Acknowledgment is accompanied by a nod of the head, subscription by a set of the mouth.

THE BOTTOM LINE

Tasks without goals are journeys without destinations.
Goals without subscriptions are promises without resolve.

14

If This Were a Perfect World

If this were a perfect world we wouldn't need performance reviews. Instead we would communicate with our employees continuously, patting them on the back when they deserve it, bopping them on the head when they deserve that. We'd give them honest and timely feedback and they'd respond with the same. There would be no secrets or surprises when performance review time came around, except for the salary-fixing part.

But this isn't a perfect world. We are not perfect employers and our employees leave something to be desired as well, where performance is concerned, anyway. Alas, the more imperfect the two of us are, the more we need performance reviews.

How important is the performance review?

How important is anything that assigns a value to someone's existence in a competitive environment? In an environment where an employee spends 45 percent of his or her waking hours? In an environment that feeds the ego as well as the family?

The performance review provides an assessment of the past year of our employees' working lives, at the same time providing direction for their next year. And if that isn't important, then breathing isn't, either.

Most important, the performance review puts a wrap on our annual employee appraisal process. It's the Oscars or the Lampoon awards, behind closed doors.

If we are serious about the notion of our people being our most valuable asset, then performance reviews rank in the upper 10 percent of our most important managerial responsibilities. And if we don't subscribe to this notion, we ought to be on the receiving end of a paycheck, instead of on the issuing end. We don't deserve the privilege of ownership.

Over my twenty-two-year entrepreneurial career I tried every make and model of performance review. The best were the individualized ones, those blank sheets of paper where I started with an intent, a few guidelines, and nothing more.

The worst were the generic ones. You know the ones I'm talking about, the forms where you check the boxes or rate an employee from one to ten, as if you were rating a prize pig at the county fair.

Sure, those generic reviews have some redeeming characteristics. They are easier and faster. And sometimes they are so easy and fast we could mail our employee a form letter and save both parties the time. Like most everything else, we get out of reviews what we're willing to put into them.

Which brings me to the basic purpose of performance reviews. First and foremost, going into the review, our intent must be to *improve the employee's performance.* Not judge his performance, mind you, but *improve it.* Everything else should be a means to that end.

Good performance reviews do not just happen. They evolve, as a result of a well-defined and thorough process. Let's take a look at the components of a successful review process:

1. Performance Expectations: Before we can conduct a meaningful review, we must first have meaningful standards by which to measure performance. Those meaningful standards are the performance expectations wherein we define the position, its responsibilities, and our expectations. (See chapter 12.)

2. Goals: Working with our employee, we must establish, and agree upon, SMART goals. (See chapter 13.)

3. Ongoing Feedback: The more communications we have on a day-to-day basis, the less explosive performance reviews will be.

4. Approach: If review time is approached as a time to dump and unload, it will turn into a glorified bitch session. Feared and loathed by both sides. Always nonproductive.

5. Critical-Event Memos: Critical events in the day-to-day performance of our employee should be noted and filed in the employee's personnel file at the time they occur, to be extracted at review time, adding objective support to otherwise subjective observations.

Critical-event memos should include episodes of positive as well as negative behavior. And since reviews are intended to improve performance, the goal of dredging up the past should be to educate and motivate, not to berate and pontificate. (Remember, we earn motivational mileage far in excess of our efforts by pointing out the employee's successes as well as his failures.)

And finally, these critical-event memos will serve a useful purpose when, and if, employer and employee end up on opposite sides of the litigational table.

6. Frequency: For most of us, assuming we're decent communicators, two reviews a year are enough; the first being the annual performance and salary review, the second (six months later) a follow-up of the first. However, when communications are sparse, or extraordinary improvement is needed, then follow-up reviews should be quarterly. Even monthly.

7. Timing: I always scheduled my performance reviews around the beginning of each fiscal year. They helped set the tone for the establishment of new budgets, the arrival of new reporting periods, and the cranking up of new attitudes. It was also important that I

get myself in a review mode. A second option is to spread the reviews over the year, scheduling them on anniversary dates.

8. The Annual Performance and Salary Review: At last, the day has arrived. The main event. The time when we compare actual performance with expectations and goals. The time when we review critical-event memos, assign new wages, and agree on bonuses and perks, all the while discussing expectations and goals for the upcoming year.

If we've followed a logical progression (performance expectations, goal setting, ongoing feedback), this will be a day of anticipation. If we haven't, this will be a day of fear.

9. The Follow-up Review: Monthly, if the situation is dire enough, quarterly or semiannually otherwise. These follow-up reviews should be informal but well prepared, and intended to determine progress since the annual review.

Thus the employee evaluation process is a natural progression that begins with performance expectations and goal setting, and ends with the performance review and the follow-up review. The performance review itself is but one piece of the process: without the other pieces the evaluation is incomplete. Don't expect earthshattering results from reviews if the entire process isn't adhered to.

We alone set the tone for the success or failure of performance reviews. If we plunge into the process with the intent of improving performance, then by God, we will improve performance. If we approach reviews constructively, they will be constructive. If we prepare for them thoroughly, the experience will be meaningful— to our company, to us, and to our employees.

Here is a collection of tips on how to improve performance reviews:

1. The more input employees have in the establishment of their performance expectations and the setting of their goals, the more

likely they will be to assess their own performance accurately. Additionally, the more input they have, the fewer surprises there will be. (Surprises should be no-nos at review time.)

Also, if employer and employee share the creation of performance expectations as well as the goal-setting process, the entrepreneur's role will be relegated to furnishing the measuring tools and assisting in resolving problems. The conflict inherent in the performance review process will fade.

2. Keep expectations as short-term as possible. Measure improvement within the next reviewing period.

3. Everything can be measured—in units, time, money, or customer satisfaction. Find a way to measure as much as is practically possible. Measurement can be both a barometer and a motivator.

4. Schedule the review in advance, giving both parties plenty of time to prepare. No phones, no interruptions. Go off-site if it promises to be a stressful process.

5. Prepare for the review itself with the same thoroughness and intensity as you would for a hire. Or a fire. Remember, reviews are benchmarks in the employee's career.

6. Begin each review with a generous helping of compliments. Get things off to a positive start. Reinforce the intent of the review early—to improve the employee's performance.

7. Be sure to evaluate the employee based on the past year's performance, not just the past month's. We're talking careers here, not trends.

8. Be honest. Sugarcoating may avoid conflict, but it only postpones improvement. Become known as an honest and candid reviewer.

9. No adjectives allowed. Be specific.

10. Back up subjective comments and appraisals with objective facts and stories, pulled from critical-event memos.

11. Remember, this is a performance review, not a character review. Keep personalities out of it.

12. A tip on determining raises: Allocate a companywide salary increase budget for the upcoming year, say, 5 percent. Then give each department head (including yourself) his 5 percent allocation. If a manager exceeds that 5 percent with one employee, he or she will have to go under it with another. This process will help keep budgets in line as well as reinforce the point that mediocre performance does not warrant automatic salary increases.

13. A twist to the review process: Have the employee write his own review, then compare the two (his and yours) and discuss. I've tried this approach and it's helpful. For both parties.

And finally, a suggestion addressed to those among us with manageable egos. You know who I'm talking about, those willing to admit, and face, their shortcomings. Those eager to improve.

Turn the performance review upside down. Ask your midlevel managers to review *you*. And have their employees review *them*. Learn what all of you can do to improve *your* performance. Bottom up as well as top down.

If we've created an honest environment in our company, the upside-down review won't be difficult. If it is difficult—if our employees are unwilling to be candid, or if we are unwilling to accept their judgments—then it's time to take a long, hard look at the culture we've created.

And the person who created it.

THE BOTTOM LINE

The performance review is the Oscar (or the Lampoon) awards ceremony of the employee feedback system.

The performance review is not complete unless it (1) identifies the improvement needed, and (2) motivates the reviewee to make that improvement.

If the employee goes away mad, the review is a failure. If he goes away motivated, the review is a success.

V

Motivating and
Directing the Team

15

Visions, Missions, and Goals

Tune in to the PGA on a Sunday afternoon. Observe Lanny Links as he tees up his ball, then steps back, adjusting his visor. Watch as Lanny squints down the fairway, imagining the flight of his ball.

Lanny has a vision.

Now he approaches the ball. Fidgeting with his grip, he reminds himself, "One-piece-takeaway and don't forget to pause at the top."

Lanny has a mission.

Finally he relaxes. A last-minute softening of his grip and he's ready. He tunes out the rest of the world and focuses on only the ball.

Lanny has a goal.

Now he swings. *Kraaaack!* His ball explodes off the tee, coming to rest two hundred and fifty yards down the fairway.

Lanny's vision has become a reality.

Well, Lanny isn't the only person around who uses visions, missions, and goals. We'd better, too. But our vision won't be a ball in the fairway or a score at the end of eighteen holes, it will be a much broader picture. A vision of tomorrow, perhaps. A perception of where our company will be and what it will look like at some point in the future. Maybe five years down the road, maybe ten. Not just in sales or product, mind you, but in distribution as well. And markets, and ownership, and manufacturing capability. And whatever else we deem important to our company's survival and growth. Whatever else we include as part of our dream.

This vision of ours, intuitive in the beginning, must eventually be put in writing and shared with our key employees and superstars. After all, doesn't it make sense that they should know where they're headed if they're to be an important part of the ride?

After vision comes mission. Mission gives direction to vision. It's a road map, a yellow brick road, a plan of action that needs to be understood by, and implemented by, the entire team. Thus our mission must be defined and developed by the masses—by the same employees who will be building the roads.

The inclusion of all of our employees in the process of defining the mission has one added benefit, in addition to providing the means to manufacture the best possible plan. From employee involvement comes also commitment, always a necessary ingredient in the process of mission fulfillment.

A reminder here. Employee involvement isn't a gift, to be packaged and wrapped and opened whenever we need it. Rather, it's an employee's conditioned response that comes from the depths of our culture. A culture that must have involved its employees in the past. If involvement hasn't been an integral part of our culture before, it's not about to happen now.

This mission statement, once determined and formalized, must then be published for all employees to read and understand. Its contents should be broadcast everywhere—in newsletters and employee manuals, on bulletin boards and memos. Its message drummed into everyone—the new employee, the faithful CFO, the veterans on the production line.

The mission statement should be short and sweet, designed for quick reading and easy recall. It's a sound bite, a Pepsi commercial, a message of nuts and bolts only. No financial goals allowed, no flowery song-and-dance routines.

The mission statement itself must:

1. Provide focus
2. Define direction
3. Differentiate us from our competition
4. Communicate our niche

As visions change (and they do change, because people change and times change and environments change), missions must also change. Not too often, hopefully, as most employees need a semi-dependable fix on the future, a light that isn't always flickering.

And finally, after the vision has been articulated and the missions have been published, we're ready to set our goals. Company goals and departmental goals and personal goals. Goals—a collection of short-term objectives that, when added together, contribute to the achievement of missions. Six-month goals perhaps, and never more than a year. Goals that are achievable and goals that, when individually accomplished, add up to a sum that is greater than its parts.

See how the combination works? Our visions beget missions that lead to our goals.

It's true in business and it's true in golf.

THE BOTTOM LINE

Visions, missions, and goals must always be subject to change. A company's only sacred cows are its principles and beliefs.

While visions, missions, and goals are necessary and fruitful, they alone don't make the difference. It's the enactment that counts.

16

Resolving Performance Problems

True story.

My twelve managers and I were cloistered in a hotel meeting room below the red and purple bluffs of Sedona, Arizona. It was our annual managers' conference and I'd hired a management consultant to teach us those things that don't come naturally to untrained small-business managers. Our annual sales growth had exploded in the past two years and our management expertise had been stretched paper thin.

The subject on this particular day was how to resolve performance problems. Probably another formula, I mumbled to myself, at the prospect of this latest attempt to resolve our problems of too much growth, too fast.

I, the eternal doubter. I, who always thought that people performed, or didn't perform, because of what was in their bellies, not what was on their bosses' minds. I, who thought that performance, like love, came from the inside, not from the outside. Your heart either wanted to do it, or it didn't.

Take Lisa, for instance. The manager of our San Francisco location, she was one of the world's truly nice people, intelligent, caring, and she understood the mechanics of our business from top to bottom. Oh yes, and she could never seem to deliver, a fact she acknowledged, and a fact that puzzled us both.

I decided I would apply today's performance-resolving lessons to Lisa. (She was in attendance, too.)

"Who has an employee performance problem they can't resolve?" the consultant began dutifully. Everyone raised his hand. Performance shortfalls seem to pervade everyone's domain.

"All right," he continued, "is this problem worth taking the time to resolve?"

It was, the thirteen of us agreed communally, nodding our heads. After all, if employees are our number one asset, how could their performance not be worthy of our time?

"And why doesn't your employee's performance measure up?" the consultant asked. "Is it because he is not able or not willing?"

"Not able," I whispered to myself, glancing at Lisa. She was certainly willing, and was as frustrated by her inability to deliver as I was.

"First let's discuss 'not willing,' " he went on, oblivious to my problem with Lisa. (Isn't that like a consultant, always saving the relevant stuff for last.) I listened anyway. I have my share of not-willings on the payroll, too.

"There are three questions to ask before you can improve a not-willing's performance," the consultant went on. "Number one, is your nonperformer getting ongoing, timely feedback from you?"

Ongoing, timely feedback? Hey, I've got twelve other people to worry about. And I've also got cash flow problems, I'm in the process of hiring a new CFO, our inventory is out of control, and our receivables need work. I have a hard enough time finding time to spend with employees who do perform, let alone those who don't.

"The second question to ask," the consultant continued, "is, is that person accountable for his performance? Or, stated another way, are there consequences for nonperformance? If the answer is no, then it's the manager's job to define the employee's accountability [via performance expectations], spell out the consequences, and agree upon a time frame for correction."

73

Accountable? Consequences? Like I said, Mr. Consultant, I've been busy. Besides, Lisa is a friend. How could I spell out painful consequences to her?

"Question number three: Are there obstacles to your employee's success? If so, it's your job to remove them."

Of course there are obstacles. But I can't be everywhere at the same time. What about our inventory and receivables and . . .

"Once you've established your feedback process, removed the obstacles, and established accountability," he went on, "the next step is to give your not-willing employee goals to achieve, a time frame to improve, and then begin the follow-up process. And then, when the agreed-upon time arrives, determine whether or not there's been a positive change by comparing his performance to his goals. If there has been a positive change, you reinforce and reward the improvement, then move forward by establishing a new set of goals. If there hasn't been, you begin the disciplinary process."

What disciplinary process?

"And one final point," the consultant intoned, looking directly at me. "Don't tell me you're too busy to improve your employee's performance. If that's what you're thinking, then you don't really believe that employees are your number one asset."

Touché.

"Now let's talk about the employee that's willing but not able. Three questions again. Number one, does your not-able have the background to achieve what's expected of him? If he doesn't, it's your job to provide the means for formal training. Classes, books, consultants."

Oops. Lisa, like the rest of us, was new to the management demands associated with the rapid sales growth we had been experiencing.

"Number two, does your not-able employee have the prerequisite experience? If not, it's your job to arrange for coaching and assistance."

Double oops. Lisa came up through our company's ranks. As in most small businesses, training had never been a priority for us. (Costs too much, takes too much time away from the job.)

"Number three, does your employee understand how to apply his experience and skills to the duties you've assigned him? If not, it's your job to arrange for on-the-job training, as well as for someone to help him work through his day-to-day management applications."

Triple oops. That someone should be me and I've been too busy.

"From there you must work with the employee to develop goals to achieve and a time frame within which to achieve them. Then begins the follow-up process. And when the time comes for review, determine whether or not the goals you've set have been achieved. If they have, reinforce his performance. If they haven't, begin the disciplinary process."

The following morning Lisa and I met for breakfast. Her mood was expectant and willing. She wanted to deliver as much as I wanted her to.

For the next six months I made Lisa number one on my to-do list. We talked on the phone several times a day. I spent the better part of a month in San Francisco working with her, removing her obstacles. And following up. We established a training program for several of her managers. She took night school courses, read books, and subscribed to a handful of management and small-business magazines.

Well, Tampa Bay could have won the Super Bowl and it would have been less of a turnaround. Lisa turned into a star of the brightest magnitude in those six months, proving once again that Deming was right. It *is* management that makes the difference.

Lisa's megawatt turnaround was the biggest victory of my fledgling management career, a miracle to behold. Except that it wasn't a miracle at all, it was a consultant's formula. A step-by-step, by-the-numbers formula designed to improve employee performance. All Lisa needed was for me to assume my end of the deal—the training, coaching, and removing of obstacles—and she would take care of the rest.

Six more months went by and San Francisco became the second most profitable location (out of six) in the company. And pushing number one.

Lisa and I have gone our separate ways in the intervening years, and I'm not sure what those years of perspective have done to her view of the experience. But I know what it's done to mine.

I've learned that victories like the one she and I shared are what make management profitable. And fun.

THE BOTTOM LINE

Most employees want to perform. It's the entrepreneur's job to provide them with the proper tools and a friendly environment.

Training + Coaching + On-the-Job Feedback = Improved Performance. Every time.

17

They Won't
Sell Widgets

Ask the typical start-up entrepreneur to show you his employee manual and he'll look as if you just asked to see his following month's cash flow projections. Or his backup financing commitment. Or his long-range strategic plans.

He won't have any.

But he ought to have all four. Especially the employee manual, a document that should be completed the same day his lease is signed. The same day his office plants are delivered. The same day his first employee is hired.

OK, so maybe employee manuals won't sell widgets. And they won't spit out mailing lists either, or manufacture products, or put smiles on the faces of customers. And, I'll admit, the process of compiling an employee manual is something akin to buying a half-dozen term life insurance policies. Not exactly steeped in excitement.

Too bad. We must compile an employee manual anyway, and make it required reading for all of our employees, old and new.

Behold what an employee manual can do. It can:

1. Get new hires started on the right foot. Set the tone for what's to come, an organized tone, a definitive tone, an accountable tone.

(Imagine the message a well-prepared employee manual sends, when a newly hired employee's questions are answered in an organized and premeditated way. Conversely, imagine the message sent when they aren't.)

2. Provide an early opportunity to publicly define your corporate missions and goals.

3. Save time later on. Time spent resolving problems that established policies would have resolved in the first place. Time spent defining those policies, as well as settling disagreements and improving damaged morale. And time spent explaining vacation days and sick days and termination policies and . . .

4. Save money (on lawyers), as well as skin (off our back), when our most important and valuable asset suddenly turns into our most incessant and burning headache.

Are we agreed, then, that assembling an employee manual is a necessary part of the motivating and directing process? Good, then get busy and find a model to build one from, a model that can be adapted to your needs. Either borrow an existing manual from someone who has already compiled one or head for the software store. (As for everything else, there's a program available.)

When compiling an employee manual, always be sure to:

1. Include a statement of visions, missions, and goals. Make it brief, make it specific, and put it up front where it's sure to be read.

2. Declare early on that the employee manual is not a legal document. And that it can, and undoubtedly will, change.

3. Don't forget to include an equal opportunity statement.

4. Spell out the benefits you offer. Health insurance, maternity leave, memberships, pensions, profit-sharing or 401(k) plans. Include the details of the health insurance plan as an attachment.

5. Define policies concerning the workday. Also include over-

time pay, time off, and breaks. As well as policies concerning performance reviews, promotions, and wage increases.

6. Include paid holiday and vacation policies.

7. Develop drug and alcohol policies, including pre-employment screening, and post-accident testing (if any).

8. Include causes for disciplinary actions and termination, and severance pay policies.

9. Be sure to keep the employee manual current, assuring that employees are aware of changes as soon as they are made. Post any changes on the bulletin board at the same time you're handing out the additions and revisions to every employee.

10. And don't forget about sexual harassment. It's a hot topic these days. Consult an attorney for the message you need to convey.

I'm the first to admit that it isn't easy to get impassioned on the subject of employee manuals, especially early on, when the start-up adrenaline is running strong. Customers and financing and new products are always more pressing. And more fun.

But persevere anyway. Employee manuals are preventative medicine in its purest form. Like novocaine and prenuptial agreements, they'll save a lot of pain later on.

THE BOTTOM LINE

If you were a new employee, wouldn't you want a written explanation of the policies and procedures surrounding your new job?

Besides answering specific questions, the employee manual brings legitimacy and professionalism to the hiring process.

18

What You Do Know Can Help You

"No, no, a thousand times no," I shouted. "I don't want to be psychologically tested."

"But Jim," my recently hired consultant reasoned, "this isn't a psychological test, it's the Meyers-Briggs Type Indicator test."

"I don't care if it's the Colgate-Palmolive College Entrance Exam," I screamed. "Shrinks cost a thousand bucks an hour and every one of them is nuttier than a case of peanut brittle."

"But Jim," he said, patting me on the head. "The Meyers-Briggs only costs fifty dollars a person and you don't have to talk to a shrink. All you do is fill out a questionnaire."

"But I don't want to know what's wrong with me," I moaned. "What I don't know won't hurt me."

"But Jim," the consultant said, "what you do know can help you."

For once, logic prevailed. Eight of my key managers, fifteen of my salespeople, and I took the Meyers-Briggs Type Indicator test.

And I've never learned more in my life. About people and employees, anyway. And about me.

Please understand that the primary purpose of the Meyers-Briggs Type Indicator test is not to change our behavior (although it will). Its primary purpose is to promote understanding among those people who take it—understanding between managers and managers, managers and employees, and employees and employees.

Here's an overview of how the Meyers-Briggs Type Indicator works:

Everybody favors one or the other in each of the following four pairs of personality traits. We're either:

Extroverted (E) or Introverted (I)
Sensing (S) or Intuitive (N)
Thinking (T) or Feeling (F)
Judging (J) or Perceiving (P)

The four choices the test tells us we favor indicate the way we act, respond, and appear to others.

Once we understand and learn to recognize each of these personality traits, the next step is to combine them into categories that fit every individual. Sixteen possible combinations result and then it's off to mixing, matching, and understanding what those combinations are and what they mean: ISTJs or ENFPs, ESFJs or ISTPs. And, lo and behold, these mixtures result in their own unique sets of personality traits.

As a result of taking the Meyers-Briggs test we are able to identify our four dominant traits at the same time our employees are identifying theirs. Subsequent aftertest debriefing will then help us to understand the underlying characteristics behind our personalities. The same with our employees. Given this shared knowledge and understanding, it follows that we will better be able to manage them. And they will better be able to be managed by us. The bottom line? A more compatible team.

Me? I was an INFP, a combination of traits that (not surprisingly) makes for good entrepreneurs and lousy managers. Meanwhile, my sales manager was an ESFJ (the quintessential sales manager), while my CFO was a bona fide INTJ (no wonder the two didn't get along).

Once I understood the personality differences between the two I could begin to resolve the conflict that always seemed to surround them. Knowing those differences and understanding the reasons behind them—not only the "whys," but the "whats"—contributed to a newfound expertise at conflict resolution.

We further learn from the Meyers-Briggs test that there are no good or bad employee types, only different ones. One employee's strength, we come to realize, is another employee's weakness. My INTJ CFO, for instance, would make a terrible sales manager. (How many introverts excel at sales?) My ESFJ sales manager would make a horrible CFO. (How many extroverts count beans with any accuracy?) There's a place in our company for everyone, and the Meyers-Briggs helps us find that place. And put the right people in it.

And then? Unless we're complete dunderheads, understanding those personality types translates into increased effectiveness in managing our team. In avoiding unnecessary conflict, resolving existing conflict, and getting things done.

Oh yes, and there's one additional benefit of the Meyers-Briggs, for those of us who have a life to live away from the office. Its lessons apply to the outside world as well.

If you want to know more than you could ever need to know about these eight personality traits, read *Type Talk at Work* by Otto Kroeger and Janet Thuesen (Delacorte, 1993). It's 398 pages of INFJs and ESTPs, ISTPs and ENFJs, ESFPs and ISTJs. (How anyone can write 398 pages on eight letters, I'll never know. But the book is available in paperback and at least worth skimming.)

For example, we further learn that if our CFO is an S (Sensor) he will "prefer specific answers to specific questions. When he asks for the time, he prefers the answer 'three fifty-two' and becomes irritated when it comes to him as 'a little before four.' " There are ten similar examples of personality traits under the Sensor category alone, and a similar number under the other seven traits. Put them together and we can't help but understand what makes bean counters the way they are. (Or sales managers. Or entrepreneurs.)

And then we can tell our CFO it's eight minutes after two whenever he asks. Everyone comes away happy.

Last but not least, *Type Talk at Work* delves into the subject of relationships. How INJPs can work with ESTPs. How ESTPs can manage ISFPs. How ISTJs can relate to ESTPs. Everyone is buried in those 398 pages somewhere. Some of us just take a little time to locate.

Taking, and understanding, the Meyers-Briggs Type Indicator test was a giant step forward for me. It helped me get my sales manager and my CFO working together. It helped me understand my art director, whom nobody could ever understand. It helped me understand why Harry could sell, why Sally couldn't spell, and why Frank could never sit still.

My advice? Take a chance. And the test. There's nothing to lose except a few hundred bucks and an hour or so of your (and your employees') time. The marketing department won't become any less creative, the accounting department won't forget which side of the ledger the debits go on, and the sales force will still ask for the order. There aren't any downsides.

But there are plenty of upsides and I'm handing out guarantees here. I guarantee that, as a result of taking the Meyers-Briggs Type Indicator test, we will have:

- Increased patience with people unlike ourselves
- Increased acceptance of personality differences
- Increased understanding, of us-and-them situations, and of them-and-them situations
- A new arsenal of leadership and management techniques
- Improved personal relationships, at home and away

Just think. All of this. And no shrink.

THE BOTTOM LINE

True understanding comes from inside. The Meyers-Briggs is an
X ray of people's personalities.

There are no good or bad employee types. Only differences.
There is a place for everyone if the entrepreneur takes the time
to look.

19

Reach Out
and Stroke
Someone

I'm from the old school. That's where a boot in the butt worked better (or so it was believed anyway) than a pat on the head. Three and a half years in the military had something to do with that, I suppose. Maybe my parents did, too.

The boot as a motivational tool hung around in my managing repertoire long after I founded my first company. Long after it should have. Take performance reviews, for instance.

I'd lie in wait for my next nonperformer like Wile E. Coyote lurking for the Road Runner. All the while remembering all the little things he'd done wrong, forgetting those he did right.

The results were predictable. My roadrunning employees came out of those reviews running faster than ever and I was the one who got beat up. And the reviews did neither or us any good.

Now don't me wrong, I'm not Wile E. Coyote by nature. Conflict is not high on my favorite-things-to-do list, and I don't enjoy censuring anyone. To the contrary, I'd much rather compliment than berate, and I far preferred those upbeat reviews that concluded with handshakes and smiles.

It took me a while but I finally learned the principle of praise.

Stroking puts Road Runners in overdrive; the boot jams them in reverse.

Unfortunately, this concept of motivation by gratification is foreign to too many of us. That's because most entrepreneurs get their gratification from within, which is one of the reasons we selected this lonely career in the first place. We get our jollies from our achievements, not from somebody else's words.

There is one more inbred trait that we have working against us, where understanding the value of stroking is concerned. For those of us who are introverts (and the majority of entrepreneurs are), the act of giving or receiving stroking doesn't come naturally. Personally, I squirm uncomfortably in stroking's presence and have been known to sweat through two shirts and a sport coat when it's aimed in my direction.

But 70 percent of our employees are extroverts, if national averages are any indication, and extroverts thrive on the gratification that comes from stroking. Which makes it our job to see that they get plenty of it, for, as with vacations and coffee breaks, most employees don't get enough. The more the merrier where stroking is concerned.

Here are a few tips on the joys of positive reinforcement:

1. Instead of spending your time looking for mistakes, look for something that's been done right. Then make a beeline for those responsible and don't be hesitant to celebrate spontaneously.

2. Broadcast the good news as well as the bad. And always find someone to blame when good news strikes.

3. Set stroking goals. At least two a day. Maybe three or four. If four o'clock comes around and the day's quota hasn't been met, get out of the office and stalk a potential strokee.

4. Stroke everywhere and anywhere. On the production line, in their office or yours, in newsletters, on bulletin boards, at

Christmas parties, and alongside water coolers. Hold official stroking meetings to celebrate the really good stuff. Become the king or queen of the stroke.

5. Overdue strokes lose their impact. Make the stroking timely, while the news is still fresh.

6. Make sure that public stroking is loud enough for all to hear. Shower it on all departments and all employees. Don't reserve it only for managers or peers.

7. Use objective, clearly defined criteria for public stroking. Criteria that are understood by, and within reach of, every employee.

8. Strive to make stroking a part of your corporate culture. Encourage all employees to stroke, not just your supervisors. Stroking can be bottom up as well as top down. There's nothing wrong with a line employee walking into the boss's office and saying, "Thanks for a job well done."

Oh yes, and one final point on the subject of positive reinforcement. A side effect of my revelation on the benefits of stroking was that those performance reviews, previously laden with conflict and stress, eventually became quite productive. Even fun.

So much fun, in fact, that I took the stroking idea home with me. Tried it on the kids. Worked there, too.

THE BOTTOM LINE

When stroking, there's a fine line between understatement and pouring it on. When in doubt, pour it on.

The more creative and immediate the stroking, the longer it is remembered.

20

The Real Oscar
Isn't Money

By the time I sold my fourth and final company, we had seventeen commission salespeople on our payroll. Good ones, too, if five consecutive years of 30 percent sales increases were any indication.

At the end of every fiscal year we hosted an annual sales seminar in Minneapolis. This seminar was a time for training, sharing of ideas, introduction of new products, and, of course, the highlight of any sales year, those hallowed year-end achievement awards. Our version of the Oscars.

Our sales Oscar was an inscribed plaque. These plaques varied in size and perceived prestige, based on dollars sold. A million dollars in sales earned the salesperson a silver plaque; $2 million, gold; $3 million, platinum; and $4 million, krypton, with $500,000 stops in between. (Don't ask me what comes after krypton. We never got that far.)

Each year a whirlwind of energy would envelop our sales department as the date for the sales seminar approached. Our offices resembled Filene's Basement during those days, as our salespeople trampled everything in their path in a frenzy to cram their last-minute orders through the system before the year officially ended.

They were piranhas attacking hamburger—to the strong went the packing slips, to the weak went the postponed sales. Along with another year of obscurity.

I remember the first time I observed this last-minute frenzy. At the time I thought I was watching just another month-end push, the sales folks' last-second efforts to assure themselves of a healthy commission check the following month. After all, I was no dummy. Salespeople are motivated by money.

Like hell they are.

Salespeople aren't motivated by money. At least the good ones aren't. They're motivated by what money keeps track of. Pure and simple, they have a burning desire to beat the other salespeople's socks off. To sell them under the table. And along come those year-end Oscars and three hundred sixty-five days' worth of sales efforts are crammed into those puny awards. Small wonder mayhem prevails.

All for that little plaque.

And it's like that for many of our nonsales employees, too, except the pursuit is not quite so intense. (Salespeople have an intensity to achieve that most other employees don't. That's why they're salespeople.) Money isn't their number one motivator, either. It's the announcement of their achievement that counts.

Make no mistake about it, recognition is the average employee's number one motivator, with money a distant fifth on the list. Here's how the progression of motivators works:

1. Appreciation-recognition
2. Feeling like part of the team
3. Getting help with personal problems
4. Security
5. Money
6. Interesting work
7. Opportunity
8. Loyalty to company
9. Working conditions
10. Discipline

How about us entrepreneurs? What would our number one motivation be if we were so polled? Wouldn't number seven on the employees' list—"opportunity"—be number one on our list? (The lesson here? Don't confuse what motivates us with what motivates our employees. There's a world of difference between the two.)

Given that our appreciation for an employee's achievement is expressed through a variety of rewards, here's a collection of tips on the subject:

1. While the reward itself may be extemporaneous, the culture surrounding rewards should be established by a definitive strategy, complete with budget and game plan.

Examine your culture when devising a reward system. What messages do you want to send? What behavior do you want to reward?

2. Don't wait for reward opportunities to appear. Go looking for them.

3. Creativity is encouraged when determining (and delivering) rewards, including, but not limited to, compensation. (The more creative the reward, the longer it's remembered.) It's OK to have controls and budgets over the reward expense category, but cut each deal to fit the employee. No two people are alike, and the effectiveness of any given reward will vary.

4. Rewards don't have to be twenty-four-karat gold to have their desired effect. They can be brass, silver, gold or, yes, even krypton. They can range from stock options to gift certificates to cash. From public thank-you's to letters of commendation to mentions in the company newsletter.

But whatever reward is used, be sure to make it loud, timely, and delivered from the top.

5. A weak award is worse than none at all. Make it appropriate or let it go unrewarded.

Is it any surprise that appreciation should appear as number one on our employees' list? I don't think so. Isn't that one of the first lessons we're taught as a child?

"Say thank you," my mother would scold.

Thirty years later her message finally sank in.

THE BOTTOM LINE

Compensation may not be an employee's number one motivator, but when a competitor wants to steal a good one, compensation is usually his foot in the door.

Dollars spent on rewards and appreciation are not an expense. They are an investment.

VI

Creating
a Flexible
Culture

21

It's a
Life-or-Death
Matter

Some say corporate culture is soft, gray, and fuzzy. They say you can't touch it, or feel it, or see it, it's just there.

Baloney. Not only can you touch culture, and feel it, and see it, you can smell it. I can smell culture the minute I drive into an office parking lot and see a Mercedes or a Jaguar parked in management's reserved parking stalls. The minute I walk into the reception room and I'm soothed by a cascading waterfall while being greeted by Vanna White's sister. The minute I'm told to pull up a chair in the waiting room because Mr. Pinkyring is "tied up on a long-distance call." The minute I walk into Pinkyring's office and imagine I've stumbled into Buckingham Palace instead.

Visit Wal-Mart's headquarters and you'll know what I mean. Sam Walton's office may be unoccupied these days but you can smell and touch and feel the culture he established, from the shiny linoleum floors to the inexpensive metal desks. His stamp is on everything and will be for decades to come.

What is this "culture" thing, anyway?

Culture is a company's value system. It's learned behavior, handed down from one year to the next, from one employee to the next. It begins at the entrepreneur's desk and ends on the shipping dock, and affects everything in between. It's a company's culture that provides the framework for defining what's acceptable behavior and what's not, from the way the coffee is perked to the way the customers are perceived.

So where do we find corporate culture?

Everywhere. In the parking lot, around the copy machine, in the local pub after the workday is done. It's in the way our employees dress, in the hours they work, in the way they solve their problems. We can watch corporate culture walk in the front door in the morning and be shipped out the back door at night.

Nothing escapes culture's grasp. It's unwritten law, defining what's done and what isn't done, what's good and what's bad, what's right and what's wrong. And if culture is the unwritten law in the company, that makes the entrepreneur the unwritten judge. The establishment of culture is like a dictatorship: it begins and ends at the top.

Here are several culture-setting tips:

1. Your company's culture begins either the day you open the door or your first day on the job, whichever comes first. And the culture that evolves will come as a result of your actions and how your employees *perceive* them. (Not how you *intend* that they perceive them.)

If you pinch pennies, your employees will pinch them, too. Spend wildly? Make way for spacious mahogany desks. Worship the customer? Ditto with your employees. Care less about quality? Watch mediocrity flourish.

Culture permeates everything your company does. It's a snapshot of you.

2. Culture starts and ends at the top. Only the entrepreneur establishes and fosters his company's culture. And only the entrepreneur changes it.

3. When it comes to culture, what you do always overrides what

you say. As a matter of fact, words not followed up by actions have an adverse effect on culture, destroying credibility in the process.

Either back up actions with words or don't speak those words in the first place.

4. Strive for balance in establishing culture. Heroes know no departments.

If you are biased toward one area of your business yourself, whether as a result of background, education, or belief, a cultural imbalance is likely to evolve.

Recognize that imbalance. Correct it. And if you can't correct it yourself, hire a counterweight to give you a hand. Someone to offset your imbalance. Someone to help you establish cultural equilibrium.

5. Got a culture you don't like? Then change it. But slowly, methodically, deliberately. It takes years to establish cultures. And they refuse to be altered overnight.

6. Everybody's culture needs a change, sooner or later. Everybody's. Consider IBM, Japan, the U.S. government. Adversity takes its toll.

Your company's culture will need a change, too, if it doesn't already. Tomorrow's events will dictate it.

7. Out of all of culture's various elements, the two most frequent errors are the fostering of a culture that (*a*) doesn't allow mistakes, and (*b*) doesn't embrace, and thrive on, change.

Allowing mistakes and welcoming change were luxuries twenty years ago. Today they're necessities.

8. The acquisitional entrepreneur should not underestimate the difficulty in changing the culture of an acquired company. The road to change will take twice as long as planned, and casualties will be twice as heavy. Go slow.

9. Inventory your culture from time to time. Take a poll, ask

your employees to write down how they perceive it. What's right, what's wrong, what needs to be changed?

Pick categories you believe to be meaningful. See how they are perceived. (Be sure to include quality, ethics, teamwork, expense awareness, leadership, concern for the customer, and concern for the employee.)

My fourth company, may it rest its weary head in peace, paid the ultimate price for its new owner's blunder in the culture-establishing process. Alas, the buyer tried to change its culture with a fist instead of a smile. Overnight instead of over time. Fatal mistakes, both.

Culture, I've learned from observing its passing, is a life-or-death matter. It kills or it instills, and it flows off the boss's desk and out of his office door like the Mississippi River following a downpour.

Meanwhile, the employees are busy controlling the floodgates. If the examples we set are the right ones, the company will float, to swim again. If they aren't, the company will drown. Like mine did.

THE BOTTOM LINE

Cultures aren't dictated and assigned, they're observed and absorbed. Observed and absorbed as a result of the entrepreneur's living example, day after relentless day, until finally they're a part of the infrastructure, defining products, employees, and management alike.

Cultures must change. If you always do what you've always done, you'll always get what you've always gotten.

From the Holy Roman Empire to the USSR, all cultures will change. Yours will, too.

22

Ten Times Better Than One

The year was 1976. My company was on a roll. Our niche was secure, our sales were exploding, and, yes, my management skills were stretched paper thin.

For once in my life I decided to seek help. I gathered my sales manager, art director, and operations manager, anointed them as our official management committee, empowered them with as much decision-making authority as I could muster, and off the four of us stumbled into the world of participatory management. If I was going to submerge myself in the sinkhole of management, I concluded, I wouldn't go down alone.

Well, I didn't go down alone. As a matter of fact, I didn't go down at all.

What happened was *we* went up. And in the process of going up I learned that four minds together think better than one, and four people together lead better than one, and four people "empowered" together manage better than one.

Did I say better than one? Make that five times better than one. Maybe ten.

OK, so I'm aware that empowerment is one of today's trendiest, most popular buzzwords. Unlike so many other buzzwords, however, it's a meaningful one, one that has long-term staying power. But staying power alone isn't enough. Empowerment by itself won't turn our frogs into princes.

What else is needed?

First, the right culture. A culture that encourages the assignment of, and acceptance of, accountability. For if we can't, or won't, hold our employees accountable, or if they can't, or won't, be held accountable, there's no possible way we can empower them. Empowerment and accountability—one needs the other to survive.

Second, empowerment needs the proper mixture of employees. No matter how much we empower our employees, it will never replace hiring and training and motivating in the entrepreneur's repertoire of daily duties. Nor will it ever be capable of turning inferior employees into superior ones. But if we have a collection of competent employees to begin with, empowerment can turn them into a team of great ones.

Funny thing. Most employees prefer to be empowered, given the choice of empowerment over abandonment, or neglect, or whatever the antithesis of empowerment is. That's why the individual benefits of empowerment, when combined with the company's benefits, result in a win-win proposition for all.

I'll admit that empowerment is one of those soft, vague, touchy-feely words that only hints of its true meaning. It's a feel-good word, and a trendy one at that. But it's a word whose time has come, and if we don't have a culture that promotes it, we'd better get busy building one.

Here is a collection of tips on how to begin:

1. Empowerment starts in the heart. If you don't feel that your employees can be or should be empowered, then empowerment won't occur.

2. The ultimate goal of empowerment should be to allow each person to contribute to his fullest capacity.

3. Empowerment requires a receptive culture in which to exist. Don't expect it to thrive if you don't have a culture that is empowerment-friendly in the first place.

An empowerment-friendly culture must:

- Hold people accountable
- Allow mistakes
- Welcome change
- Encourage new ideas and participation
- Allow delegation of responsibility
- Be flexible

4. Empowerment is only successful when the right raw materials are in place. Which means if you don't have empowerable employees you must first change your hiring qualifications. And increase your commitment to training. And motivate your employees better, and compensate them more creatively, and . . .

5. People need to be given a voice before they'll accept the responsibility of empowerment. So, give them that voice—in the decision-making process, in setting their goals (and rewarding them), and in defining their roles. And while you're at it, give them a voice in the hiring process as well, and in directing the development of your culture, and in determining missions and strategies.

6. Successful empowerment requires understanding from the empoweree, and the surest way to build that understanding is through sharing. Sharing of the entrepreneur's vision, of his responsibilities, and yes, of his sacrosanct financial statements.

It's the age-old story. People don't want to be handed the reins unless they're familiar with the horse.

7. Beware when in an empowering mode. Not everyone wants to be empowered. There are plenty of capable employees in the world who want nothing more than to assemble their widgets, send out their invoices, and sweep the floors at night. Leave them alone or take extra precautions.

8. And one final point. What better way to empower employees than to share equity. That's empowerment with a capital *E*.

I'm not advising that equity be given away, but rather that it be rewarded away, in the form of bonuses for services rendered. Parcel it out, in small pieces over long periods of time. (Besides the benefits of increased motivation, the sharing of equity has no negative effects on the balance sheet or cash flow.) Nor am I suggesting giving away more than 49 percent, unless it's the entrepreneur's time to move over or move on.

Why, this issue of employee ownership is so obvious these days, it's even encouraged by the U.S. government, in the form of ESOPs. What's more (for once Uncle Sam's intentions and actions are in agreement), there are a number of tax reasons why ESOPs make sense.

In the final analysis, there is only one thing that stands in the way of successful empowerment: the entrepreneur's ego. When we think we're the only one who can do the job. Who can make the decision. Who can accept the responsibility.

And remember, the number one key to successful empowerment is the empowerer. That's us. It's up to us to assemble a team capable of being empowered.

THE BOTTOM LINE

Empowerment without accountability is like training without follow-up. A prelude to waste.

If your employees aren't empowerable, you should ask yourself why.

Empowerment may utilize a team, but it will never develop one. Hiring, training, and motivating come first.

23

Secrets Are
for Lovers Only

The following scene really happened. Pull up a chair.

ENTREPRENEUR (*moaning softly*): God, my employees make
me mad!
GRIZZLED VETERAN: How so?
ENTREPRENEUR: They've got this thing about salespeople.
For some reason they hate their guts. (*Shrugs helplessly.*)
They just don't understand.
GRIZZLED VETERAN: What don't they understand?
ENTREPRENEUR: They don't understand they wouldn't have
jobs if it weren't for salespeople.
GRIZZLED VETERAN: That so?
ENTREPRENEUR (*rolling his eyes*): That's so. Hell, old-timer,
everyone knows that the success of every business begins
with the sale. Nothing happens until a sale is made.
Cut!

All right, readers, now you tell me. If you were the Grizzled
Veteran, what would be your response to Mr. Entrepreneur?
Hmmmmmmm.

Well, not tooooo bad. But here's mine:

Sorry, Mr. Entrepreneur, but everybody *doesn't* know that nothing happens until a sale is made. How can they know unless someone has taken the time to enlighten them?

And anyway, what can you expect of your employees where their attitudes toward salespeople are concerned? After all, salespeople (1) make *x* times as much money as everyone else, (2) wear coats and ties and have air-conditioned offices, (3) are always trying to tell us how our products *should* be made, and (4) aren't chained to their offices like the rest of us.

I mean, how can a nonsales employee *not* be expected to have a thing about salespeople?

Unless, that is, someone enlightens those nonsalespeople. Unless someone educates them as to what salespeople really do. Unless someone instructs them that sales is the eyes, ears, and voice of the customer. And unless someone explains the role of the customer in the business equation.

And so it goes with anything else that our employees don't understand that we expect them to understand but that hasn't been explained. Such as:

- Our company's mission. What it is and why it is.
- Enough financial figures to make them feel that their understanding matters.
- How much we pay in taxes. How we support our community.
- Who our competitors are. What they do that we don't do and vice versa.
- What makes us unique in the marketplace.
- What happens when a lousy product is delivered.
- The reason behind a recent investment. Or expenditure.
- The reason behind a recent success. Or failure.
- Whatever else we assume they already know, but they really don't. Or whatever else we have previously determined they don't need to know, but they really do.

Running an "open" company is today's buzzword for this phenomenon of employee enlightenment. I'd call it common sense.

What's in it for us? The behavior we seek from our employees, for one thing. And their trust for one other.

And what's in it for our employees? The opportunity to feel that they're part of the team. And the caring that comes from that feeling.

See how it works? Everyone wins.

And what if our employees don't buy whatever it is we've just enlightened them with? Then either we've done a poor job of explaining it, or it doesn't make any sense in the first place, or we've hired the wrong employees.

See what I mean? It's never *them*. It's always *us*.

Which means it's time for us entrepreneurs to get off our duffs and teach our employees what salespeople really do. And whatever else they ought to know.

There are a myriad of ways to enlighten employees:

- In the employee manual.
- In newsletters.
- Hold an employee meeting. (We're quick to hold shareholders' meetings, why not jobholders' meetings?)
- Make a video if employees aren't all under one roof.
- Meet with new hires and take the time to explain the message.
- Post it on the bulletin board.
- Make a sign for the lunchroom.
- Include a flier with the paycheck.
- Have your supervisors explain the issue, one on one.
- Wander the floor. The offices. The water cooler. The copy machine.

Do something! Anything!

But don't blame your employees when they don't automatically understand how your business works. When they can't fathom the underpinnings of the culture. Or your customers, or your missions, or the visions running through your free-wheeling head.

Employees aren't mind readers or psychics, you know. They're regular folks, like we used to be, and someone must plant the seed before their knowledge can grow.

That someone is us.

Johnny Knowledgeseed.

THE BOTTOM LINE

Sell them, don't tell them. People respond best when they understand why.

Secrets may be for lovers and FBI agents, but they're not for flexible entrepreneurs.

24

A Formula
That Works

My mind goes back twenty years. Maybe more. I remember a seminar somewhere, another business speaker making his point.

"The number one mission of a manager is to hold his people accountable," the speaker intones. Memory fades.

Flip back another twenty years or so. My mother stands before me, hands on her hips. "Don't demand and you won't get," she lectures, in her Ben Franklin tone of voice.

And finally a fragment from somewhere, a magazine article perhaps. "Impatience is the father of change," come the words through a fog.

And now I understand. Thanks to the passage of time, those messages have taken root, although I never used two of them during the years of my entrepreneurial career. Oh, I was impatient enough (and still am today), but demanding? Holding people accountable? Not for this nonconflictive nice guy. No sir, not for me.

I was the Reverend Jim, Santa Claus in straight clothes, always the bearer of good tidings. I never intended to hurt anyone—their feelings, their future, or, most of all, their opinion of me. (Now I know: thin skin is the enemy of management.)

Finally, twenty years later, I can fit the pieces of the puzzle together. That long-forgotten consultant, my long-remembered mother, that fuzzy magazine article. All three spoke the truth. Each contributed a piece to another management formula that actually works.

Impatience + Demanding + Accountability = Results

Here's what I mean:

Impatience

Patience may be a virtue when raising kids, training dogs, or excavating archaeological digs, but it isn't much help when it comes to managing a business. That's when impatience becomes the virtue.

Impatience means uneasiness. Uneasiness with the way things are. A desire to see that they improve. A restlessness for change. An unhappiness with the status quo.

While it's possible to create a new business without impatience, it's impossible to manage a growing business without it. And the more our company grows and the higher up in the management ranks we rise, the more pronounced our need for impatience becomes.

That's because we have more to be impatient about. More demands on our time, more threats to our success, more people taking their shots at the victories we've achieved.

And that impatience can come from so many sources. For some it's inbred, like red hair and blue eyes. For others it comes through the influence of outsiders—bankers, shareholders, and directors. For still others it evolves as a result of previous successes (the true entrepreneur never gets enough), or in some cases, the fear of impending failure.

Wherever it comes from, our impatience serves to stimulate us, but alone it won't achieve results. That's why we also must be . . .

Demanding

Impatience, where the management of people is concerned, is caused by what employees haven't done, or by what they have done but shouldn't have. And it is only assuaged by what employees have done, and should have.

The bigger our company grows, the more we come to rely on people other than ourselves to satisfy this impatience of ours. Some of our employees will respond because of the way they are, but many must be spurred into action. Which is where the "demanding" part of the formula enters in.

"Don't demand and you won't get," my mother lectured. Remember? Well, she was right.

Sure, there's a time and a place for the warm and fuzzy approach (when we're surrounded by superstars who are capable of managing and motivating themselves), and when it works, fine. Bask in it. Warm and fuzzy is always the easiest. And the most enjoyable.

But warm and fuzzy isn't always enough, even when we've collected a team of superstars. "Demanding" is often the next step. Demanding, as in asking the tough questions and demanding the straight answers. And doing that demanding up front, before the mistakes are made, then following it up until the job gets done.

But impatience and demanding by themselves still won't solve all of our management problems. Oh, impatience will provide the impetus to resolve them and demanding will set the stage, but neither will provide the results. What will provide the results is the final piece of the management puzzle. We must direct our demands to people who are held . . .

Accountable for Their Actions

Accountability. Performance to expectations. Achievement of specified and agreed-upon goals and objectives. So simple to understand, so difficult to achieve.

Let's face it, our employees have two options when we demand something of them. Either they do it or they don't. Either they achieve or they don't. And the factors that determine whether they do or they don't?

Is there any compelling reason why they should? Does their achievement make a difference? Do they know what that difference is? Must they achieve, or is it only an option?

Go on, I dare you. Ask these questions about your company. Do you have an accountable culture?

As we discussed earlier, most employees are not motivated by the same things entrepreneurs are. Achievement is not at the top of their list, which doesn't make them wrong, only different. It's our role to introduce an element that, in the absence of this self-motivation, compels them to achieve.

That element is accountability. Again, it's a cultural issue, and again, it begins with us. We must hold our employees accountable to achieve whatever it is they've set out to achieve (and ensure they do the same with the employees they manage), or we go back to square one.

Engulfed by impatience again.

And that's how the management formula works. Impatience breeds demands, which, when combined with accountability, result in—results.

As with any formula, remove one of the elements and it doesn't work anymore.

Which of the three is missing in your company?

THE BOTTOM LINE

Be impatient with the status quo.
Ask tough questions, demand straight answers.
Instill a culture that holds employees accountable for achieving their goals.

25

If All Our Employees Were Like Us

Teetering near the top of most entrepreneurs' things-I-hate-to-do list is follow-up.

I mean, why should we have to follow up? We've already gotten whatever-it-was off our desk once, why must we do it all over again? What are employees for, anyway? Hell, if we were an employee, we'd never have to be followed up.

But we aren't an employee. We're an employer and there's a world of difference. (Review your loan guarantees if you're having any doubts.) And follow-up is an important part of making any management formula work, especially in the early stages of our business, when cultures are being established. Before our team of superstars is assembled.

As early-stage managers, we must learn to follow our employees up, whether we, or they, like it or not. Whether we want to or not. Whether we think it's necessary or not.

So swallow that deep-seated distaste for follow-up and do it. Because if you don't, here are the downsides that will follow:

- Demands not followed up won't be demands anymore. They'll be pleas.

- Goals not followed up won't be goals anymore. They'll be simply a matter of crossing your fingers that the job will get done.
- Customers will go elsewhere. Today's customers clamor for follow-up, and if we don't follow them up, our competitors will.
- Investments turn into expenses. Especially investments in training, which, when not followed up, turn into wastes of time and money.
- Everyone working for us stops following up, too. And soon we have an entire company of people who don't follow up. And then accountability disappears. To be followed by credibility.

Following up is only half of what it takes to establish a culture that includes accountability. (The other half is punishment. Stay tuned for the following chapter.) Once we've established the expectation of follow-up, our employees will learn to anticipate its coming. And that's when things get done.

The good news is that once our employees know that follow-up is coming, the need for it decreases. Which means once our accountable culture is in place we won't have to follow up as much anymore. We can spend more of our time on the front end of our tasks and less on the back end.

But the culture must come first!

Have you ever noticed how many activities important to the sales process are also key to managerial success? Listening and preparation and problem solving (among others) all had their origins in sales.

Well, ditto with follow-up. Show me a salesperson who doesn't follow up and I'll show you a salesperson who won't make his projections. Or his draw. And show me an entrepreneur who doesn't follow up and I'll show you an aspiring manager who won't make the transition.

In the beginning, when our corporate cultures are developing, every commitment made, large or small, must be followed up. A simple notation on the calendar followed by a transfer to the to-do list on the appropriate day should complete the process. (Following up is not brain-surgeon activity.)

But no matter how easy following up is, it will never rank up there with golf or a John Grisham novel as our favorite way to pass the time. Thus we should never stop trying to collect a team of superstars who require a minimum of it. (Superstars who consistently need follow-up aren't really superstars.)

But until that time comes, following up should be an integral part of the managing process. For us and for our managers, too. Unless they've succeeded in accumulating a team of superstars themselves, managers need to follow up their employees, too.

And remember, following up isn't the end of the commitment process. Rather, it's the beginning of the accountability process. It sets the tone for achievement and needs to be given the same back-end energy and attention given to the commitment at the front end.

What's that? Who should be following *us* up?

Why, no one, of course. But not to worry. If we need following up, we won't need it much longer.

Either our job is about to disappear, or we are.

THE BOTTOM LINE

Commitments not followed up won't be accomplished commitments. They'll be forgotten promises.

The more you follow up, the less you need to.

26

When All
Else Fails

"Spare the rod and spoil the child," my parents would shrug, before flailing away.

Well, I'm not so sure that axiom works where today's parenting is concerned (although I must admit I resorted to it occasionally), but I can vouch for its managerial counterpart: "Spare the punishment and destroy the accountability."

Now, don't get me wrong, I'm not advocating that today's entrepreneurs tote nightsticks, crunch people's heads, and carry on like the L.A.P.D. While fear may be an effective motivator on the streets of Los Angeles, it has no place in the offices of our company. And where it does exist, vibrant and healthy small businesses will not.

The entrepreneur who wishes to encourage creativity in his culture must first ensure that the element of fear is absent. And fear can only be absent when punishment is known to be tendered privately, not exercised publicly. When punishment is applied softly, not brandished forcefully. When punishment is wielded as a tool, not swung like a club.

Punishment, to be a successful motivator, should always be:

- Called upon only as a last resort
- Tendered with the intention of improving, not enforcing
- Used without rancor

It is our responsibility to assure that no punishment be meted without cause, and on those occasions when it must be meted, the cause must be duly recorded. That is to say, keep score. Write it down. Use critical-event memos, and don't forget to include the good as well as the bad.

This score-keeping exercise is intended not only to ensure that justice is ultimately served (when review time comes around) but also to keep the lawyers away. Carefully kept records of performance are our number one exhibit when it comes time to prove justifiable termination. (Remember, terminated employees don't just go away, they go away mad.)

And speaking of termination, as much as we'd like to avoid it, it has its place in the growth of a healthy business. Not often, hopefully, if we hire right, and train right, and motivate right. But it will happen. And if it doesn't occur now and then, we're bound to have a handful of nonperforming employees infiltrating our payroll, along with a culture that condones mediocrity.

It's a fact:

The weakest employees will surround the entrepreneur who procrastinates the longest when it's time to say good-bye.

Once the hire is made, our responsibility in the process of collecting potential superstars is far from over. We still must train them and motivate them and, assuming the law of averages is alive and well, sixty days after the hire we sometimes have to terminate them. (At which time our trusty entrepreneurial instincts will appear and we'll put off the *F* word for another six months or so. Or at least until our performing employees congregate outside our office to tell us it's either him or them.)

Let's face it, I doubt if even George Steinbrenner enjoys the firing process, but the timely performance of it is an integral part in our drive to surround ourselves with superstars. If we are one of those folks whose logic is dictated by the heart and not the head, here are several arguments to assist the heart in reaching the right decision:

1. The fear of being fired is worse than the event itself. No employee can perform when working under the threat of imminent termination.

2. Most employees know when they are underperforming and are as unhappy in their jobs as you are in having them there. Yet they're too afraid or insecure (or motivated by unemployment laws) to make the first move.

3. The size and frequency of opportunities available to your performing employees are adversely affected by the presence of underperforming employees. You are doing your contributing employees a gross injustice by keeping the laggards around.

4. You have an obligation to your performing team members, your shareholders, and your creditors to collect a team of superstars, not a team of benchwarmers.

5. Lighten up on yourself. You're not passing judgment on the person being terminated, but rather on his behavior in that particular job. His talents, which may be many, simply lie elsewhere.

All of which will not make the firing process the highlight of the entrepreneur's day. It may however allow us an hour or two of sleep after a tough one.

Here are several tips on the unpleasant task of firing:

1. In business as in life, postponed problems never get better, they only get worse. As soon as the decision is made to terminate, do it!

2. Explore the alternatives. Demotion, grace periods, consultant contracts. When they won't work, record the reasons why. The employee will probably ask.

3. Arrange for outplacement services.

4. When firing an old-time employee or a member of a minority, check with an attorney first.

5. Prepare the firing package in the same organized and documented way you prepare a hiring package. Include severance, health insurance, disposal of company car, duration of benefits, etc.

6. Plan the firing as if it were a business meeting (which it is). Organize in advance, outline the presentation, have handouts prepared. Make it as businesslike as possible, and, above all, avoid sentimentality and reminiscing. Keep emotions subdued; they only make matters worse.

7. Don't argue. State the reasons and the facts surrounding the termination. Show the supporting documents. Arguing won't change your mind and will only serve to incense the person being fired. Let him unload if he chooses—he might feel better when he's done.

8. When it's time to terminate, prevent a daylong buildup of fear and dread. Do it first thing in the morning.

9. Arrange the day so the firing is followed by something to take your mind off the event. A job you enjoy, perhaps, or maybe a movie, a tennis game, a jaunt with the kids.

And remember this when feeling sorry for yourself because you have to terminate someone.

It's a hell of a lot tougher on the guy across the desk.

THE BOTTOM LINE

Punishment should be regarded as a tool for improvement, not a club for enforcement.

Don't let the heart dictate to the head in matters of punishment. The entrepreneur has a responsibility to his performing employees, and the presence of underperformers encourages mediocrity, violating that responsibility.

Fear is the enemy of creativity. Don't allow it.

27

It's a Lopsided Deal

All other things being equal, when sales and accounting clash, sales usually wins. Ditto with sales and operations. And sales and administration. And sales and the FBI, and sales and the IRS, and sales and just about anybody else.

Oh sure, maybe sales loses a battle here and there, but they always win the war. That's because winning's in their genes—they're bred to prevail. That's why we hired them and that's why they make barrelfuls of money, and if they weren't in the habit of winning they wouldn't be in sales in the first place.

Which is the way it ought to be. Salespeople have to be aggressive and assertive and act like runaway steamrollers on a downhill grade. Most of the good ones I know are that way.

And they can't leave that aggressiveness out on the streets. Nor can they check it at the door or hang it in the closet alongside their coats. Instead, they bring it into the office, to be foisted on our hapless employees. And on us.

After all, our salespeople, the good ones anyway, understand how the business game works. They know that if they take a walk in the morning, their best accounts will follow in the afternoon. They long ago learned that customers maintain their relationships with salespeople, not with CFOs, COOs, or even presidents. Sorry, but our salespeople aren't dummies. They know where the leverage is.

So what? So wherever salespeople go, customers are sure to follow.

Meanwhile, when our operations, or administration, or accounting folks decide to move on, they pack up a picture or two, a calculator, and maybe a potted plant. And that's about all that goes. Then we replace them in a week or two, swallowing the cost of training and experience. An expensive departure, for sure, but rarely a fatal one.

So what? So wherever nonsalespeople go, customers don't give much of a damn.

And if that isn't enough, salespeople know they're not the commodity the rest of us are. They're a special order. A custom-made product. Good salespeople don't have to line up in front of our office, looking for jobs. We know where to find them.

In these days of corporate downsizing, however, good administrators do line up in front of our office or at least fill the mail with glittering resumés. Ditto for good accountants. And order-entry clerks. And engineers. And artists. And yes, even presidents sometimes.

And maybe this skew to sales isn't fair, but too bad. That's how the system works.

Like it or not, it's a lopsided deal. The world tilts toward sales, even though it's a cultural-imbalance issue with dangerous implications. It's a cultural imbalance that we must deal with. Softly and gently, but deal with, nonetheless.

It's our job to blend our salespeople in with the rest of the team, maintaining a sales-driven culture but keeping all of our employees content in that environment. Here are several suggestions on how to go about that process:

1. Work continually to keep sales' feet on the ground as well as their egos in check. Chip away, reminding them constantly of everything that goes into making, and keeping, customers content.

Help them to understand the role of the rest of the team along with the problems they face. Coax them, and massage them, and never let them forget that everyone has a role in keeping their customers happy.

2. Educate nonsales employees in the ways of the world, including the role of the customer in the business equation. Explain the customer's relationship with your company, as well as the customer's relationship with the salesperson. It's a difficult concept for nonsales types to accept.

Sure, products are important, but there are a lot of good products that never make it to the marketplace. In the end, it's sales and distribution that make the difference.

3. Involve nonsalespeople in the sales process, especially those in game-breaker positions. Every one of your game-breaking superstars should accompany a salesperson on a sales call at infrequent intervals. These visits give them an opportunity to meet, and interact with, real live customers, as well as to get a sobering insight into the customer/salesperson relationship.

4. Prime the cultural pump by promoting the importance of the team. Bring the salespeople in when there's a production or shipping or paperwork crisis, to work alongside a nonsales employee. Give them a glimpse of what it's like on the other side of the fence while they pitch in.

This crisis-resolution opportunity will give the rest of the employees a chance to work alongside, and better understand, the salespeople, even as the problem is being resolved.

My company always involved our salespeople in our biggest and best (and all-too-frequent) crises. Everybody—accounting, sales, administration, and of course, me—would join hands and pitch in when a good crisis came along. Those crises were proven team unifiers, and a warm glow always settled over our company after we resolved the best ones.

Like I've always said, there's nothing like a good crisis to pump up a team.

As long as they don't occur too often.

THE BOTTOM LINE

Sales is the horse; production, administration, and the rest of the team, the cart.

But all are headed in the same direction.

28

Meetings Get a Bum Rap

Meetings get a bum rap. It isn't their fault they're hated so much. It's ours. As a matter of fact, a good meeting can be a delicate piece of work, a hand-crafted, flowing, pleasurable experience.

But there's nothing worse than a bad meeting, except for maybe a Sylvester Stallone movie. Bad meetings create more problems than they resolve. Besides wasting everyone's time, they cost big money, at the same time that they're sending ominous signals to our employees.

Stop and look at the subject of meetings from our employees' point of view. If we allow schlocky meetings, they must think, what's to stop us from hiring schlocky employees, and shipping schlocky products, and running a schlocky organization? After all, schlock begets schlock.

Look around the room at the next meeting you attend. Where is time more abused? And I'm not just talking about our time, either, I'm talking about everyone's time. The meeting starts late, some folks shouldn't be there anyway, the facilitator drones on, and the meeting lasts longer than last year's Academy Awards. And there sit our finest and highest-paid employees, representing wages of hundreds of dollars an hour. Bored, eyelids flickering, drowsily sucking their thumbs. Meanwhile their In baskets languish placidly, unattended and overflowing.

Then multiply the cost of that lousy meeting by the number of other lousy meetings our company has hosted that day. Next multiply the answer by 255, the number of working days in a year. And if the sum we arrive at doesn't hurt, then neither does dropping a piano on our head.

Let's face it, if we can't manage a meeting, how can we expect to manage an entire company?

I'll warn you, this chapter is going to be a long one. I've got this thing about meetings. Meetings are in the top ten of every small business's "needs improvement" department, and they are also in the top ten of every small business's "how-we-can-make-a-huge-impact-with-a-minimum-of-effort" category. There's no excuse for not improving our meetings. None.

It isn't like we're changing a culture or improving a paper flow system or developing a new product here. Meetings aren't gray-matter exercises. They can be improved quickly and easily, with a minimum of effort. And the results can be oh-so-pleasurable. And oh-so-immediate.

Here's a process for improving meetings:

Step One:
Preparation

Make a personal decision to declare war on lousy meetings. Cast it in stone.

Several weeks before going public with your officially declared war on lousy meetings, take an inventory of the number of meetings held every day in your company, the number of attendees, and the length of the meetings. Get an idea of how much time is being spent, and wasted, in meetings.

And how much money that time represents. It doesn't take a

Cray supercomputer to tally how much money meetings cost. Take the hourly rates of the attendees (including benefits) multiplied by the time spent in the meeting, multiplied by the number of attendees. And remember to pad the time by ten minutes on either side—the time wasted going to and from the meeting.

Step Two:
Focus and Commitment

Like any other problem/opportunity that arises, you need to focus on overcoming/taking advantage of it. And I don't mean dabble with that problem/opportunity, I mean *focus* on it. And I don't mean your CFO or office manager should focus on it, I mean *you* should be doing the focusing, as your company's numero uno Meeting Revolutionary.

This isn't a long-term commitment of time you're making here; it should only take a month or two of concentrated efforts to win the war on lousy meetings. (If you can't solve this problem in two dedicated months, then you have an even bigger problem.)

So make a personal commitment to focus on improving your meetings, then allocate enough time each day to spend on it. Go to meetings (those you're invited to and those you aren't) with pen and paper in hand. Pay attention to the form of the meeting as well as the content. Observe, record, and compute. And put the war on lousy meetings on the top of your to-do list and leave it there until you're satisfied the enemy is beating a hasty retreat.

Step Three:
Announcement

Now it's time to go public with your war. Time to make the official announcement. I mean broadcast the hell out of the news—bells, whistles, bulletin boards, newsletters, memos (and yes, meetings).

Whatever it takes to let everyone know how important this project is to you. And to your company.

Most employees won't complain. They don't like lousy meetings any more than you do. They put up with them because you put up with them.

Step Four:
Training

Establish a training program (designed by you and taught by you) for all employees, facilitators and participants alike. Entire books are written on the subject of meetings. Find one, read it, and pare it to meaningful size.

Then use that information along with the tips in this chapter, to train your employees and upgrade your meetings. It isn't difficult, this improvement of meetings. Rather, it's a simple combination of focus, logic, and discipline. Managerial characteristics, all three.

Step Five:
Follow Up

Conclude the war on lousy meetings (your direct involvement, at least) with a follow-up program designed to give your employees feedback on the improvements made and the areas still needing improvement.

You should be able to delegate your war after two months. By then it should be downgraded to a police action.

OK so far?

Following is a collection of tips on how to improve your meetings, divided into five categories: the facilitator, meeting preparation, starting on time, content, and general.

Facilitator

1. A strong facilitator is the key to a successful meeting. The role of the meeting facilitator, his responsibility, and his authority should be clearly defined and understood by all employees.

2. Unless a meeting's intent is purely creative, the facilitator should be the planner, the orchestrator, and the director.

3. It is the facilitator's responsibility to see that the focus of the meeting is maintained, that the subject stays on track, and that no one dominates the discussion (unless that person is making a formal presentation).

4. The facilitator should encourage those introverted attendees to become involved at the same time he is striving to contain the extroverted ones.

5. It is the facilitator's uncompromising responsibility to see that the meeting starts, and ends, on time.

Preparation

1. The facilitator should send out a meeting notice at least one day in advance of the meeting. Include the time it begins, time it ends, location, and general subject matter. This gives the attendees advance notice, allowing them plenty of time to think about, and prepare for, the subject of the meeting. The notice should also include any preparations to be made in advance of the meeting, as well as anything the attendees need to bring.

2. Spill all the beans in the meeting notice. The fewer the surprises in the course of meetings, the better.

3. It is the facilitator's responsibility to make sure the meeting room is set up properly.

Starting the Meeting on Time

1. Tardiness is a cultural issue, and a stepchild of time management. If meetings consistently begin late it is a symptom of a greater problem and should be dealt with as a cultural issue. Meanwhile, here are some stopgap ideas on how to make attendees show up on time:

The facilitator should be five minutes early and begin the meeting religiously on time, no matter who isn't there. And then:

- charge latecomers a dollar a tardy minute, or
- make the last arrival buy doughnuts for the next meeting, or
- start the meeting without the latecomers, locking the door with them on the outside, or
- start the meeting allowing the latecomers to drift in, after handing them an invitation to the boss's office following the meeting, or
- cancel the damn meeting. And if people are late for the rescheduled meeting, cancel it, too.

2. For the first two months of the war on lousy meetings, maintain a meeting log. Record each meeting, how many people attend, the cost, whether or not it started on time, and who was late.

In most cases, the record-keeping task will solve the tardiness problem by itself. If it doesn't, we're back to the cultural problem again.

Content

1. State clearly the purpose of the meeting at the outset.

2. Set one primary goal of the meeting and make sure it dominates the agenda. Limit the additional subjects to no more than three.

3. Don't allow interruptions. Not only do interruptions disrupt the process, they send a message of relative importance. Which is to say, the meeting isn't.

4. Follow agendas closely when the meeting is informational or operational. Allow for tangents when discussing more open-ended topics such as strategy, new products, or creative directions.

5. Informational meetings should end on time. Problem-solving or creative meetings should end as close to on time as possible. Remember, the attendees have other responsibilities that are going unmet when the meeting extends beyond its scheduled time.

6. It is the facilitator's responsibility to recap and state conclusions at the end of the meeting. Leave no points unconcluded, no personal commitments overlooked.

7. Every meeting should be followed up with a memo from the facilitator spelling out the decisions reached and the personal responsibilities that have evolved.

8. End the meeting on an upkick. If there's good news to pass on, save it for last. Review and conclude on a positive, encouraging note.

General

1. This is the age of speed and sound bites. Quicker and punchier is best.

2. When in doubt, huddle in the hallway instead of having an organized meeting. Or meet informally in someone's office.

3. Know the cost of the meeting in advance.

4. Never hold meetings on Monday mornings or Friday afternoons.

5. The usefulness of most problem-solving or creative meetings is inversely proportional to the size of the group.

6. Most meetings, especially the ongoing, regularly scheduled ones, are attended by more people than necessary. Cull often and selectively.

7. Any ongoing meeting held more than once a month should be scrutinized carefully. Meetings can be habit-forming, and no meeting should be sacred. (Cash flow meetings are the exception.)

8. Most people prefer not to be invited to meetings. For those who are sensitive to being omitted, explain the criteria for attendance.

9. And finally, if anyone is spending more than 25 percent of his or her time in meetings, something is wrong with the organization chart. And the organization.

Meetings are like telephones and paperwork. They are necessary, prone to mismanagement, and always maligned by those on the using end.

And needlessly maligned, I might add, if it's us doing the maligning. For this is our company and we're in the culture establishing business, and if we don't like what's going on in our meetings (or with our telephones or with our paperwork), we're in a position to change it.

Which is the number one reason we selected this career in the first place.

THE BOTTOM LINE

Companies with time-abusing cultures are usually the same companies that conduct ineffectual meetings. The two go hand in hand.

Question the need for every meeting and for every attendee. No meeting is sacred (other than cash flow), and no attendee is indispensable.

29

Time and the Abuse Thereof

I'll be honest with you. Cellular phones bother me. You see them in too many places that telephones don't belong—on the golf course, at the ballpark, in an automobile doing 95 down the San Diego Freeway.

And cellular phones aren't the only things that bother me. Portable fax machines and pen computers and electronic Rolodexes bother me, too, as well as a zillion and one other space-age doodads whose names I can never remember. And whose functions I don't understand.

We used to light up a cigarette after a pleasurable experience. Should we now reach for a cellular phone instead?

We used to sing, "Ah, sweet mystery of life," when our emotions overcame us. Should we now send a fax instead?

We used to shout, "Olly, olly, in free," when our playmates eluded us. Should we now reach for a belt pager instead?

Where will it end?

My confusion notwithstanding, cellular phones, faxes and pagers are efficient time management tools. But as efficient as they are, it isn't hardware that will eventually solve our time management problems. It's software.

And I don't mean computer software, I mean our companies' internal software. Because, regardless of what the telecommunications ads tell us, time management isn't a technical issue. It's a cultural one.

Our management of time won't be improved one iota because of equipment alone. The attitude must come first. Ours and our employees'.

Can you imagine a professional manager worth his salt putting up with employees who don't return phone calls? Can you imagine him putting up with employees who wander into meetings fifteen minutes late? Can you imagine him putting up with an employee who wanders into the office at eight-thirty when everyone else is on the job at eight?

I can't.

Like I said, time management is a cultural issue, and it's the entrepreneur who does the culture setting. If we choose to abuse people's time—ours or somebody else's—no amount of cellular phones, faxes, or belt pagers will counteract that abuse.

If you're anything like me, time abusers rank right up there with smoke-filled restaurants and Burger King commercials in terms of popularity. Here's a sampling of the thoughts that cross my mind when someone abuses my time:

1. The abuser is telling me his time is more important than mine. (Maybe it is, but I don't have to be slapped in the face with the news.)

2. The abuser can't manage his own time, and so he's taken to wasting mine.

3. The abuser's boss, and his entire company for that matter, can't manage their time, either. If they could, the company wouldn't hire time-abusing employees. Or let them proliferate.

4. Who wants to do business with a company that can't manage its time? What else can't it manage?

How is my time abused? Let me count the ways:

1. By schedules unmet.

2. By appointments unkept.

3. By meetings that last an hour, but should have lasted ten minutes.

4. By people who come late to meetings.

5. By meetings that shouldn't be held in the first place.

6. By the telephone, in so many ways. (Long voice mail messages, phone calls not returned, ringing phones not picked up, unnecessary calls, ad nauseam.)

7. By people, damn their good intentions, who take fifteen minutes to say what could be said in five.

8. By waiting. In waiting rooms. Outside offices. For someone to get off the phone. Or off the fax, or away from the copier, or . . .

9. By someone else's errant culture—a culture that allows time abusers to proliferate.

10. Oh yes, and by authors who take 500 pages to say what could have been said in 250.

OK, so we're agreed that time abuse is a cultural issue and not conducive to efficient business management. So what should we do about it?

We can begin by encouraging a culture in our company that values time instead of abuses it. A culture that:

• Requires people to be on time. For the opening bell in the morning, for meetings, conferences, and whatever. (A salesperson who is always late would be out of a job in a heartbeat. Why should the rest of us be any different?)

- Never holds a meeting, when a conversation around a desk would suffice.
- Requires informational meetings to be quick and to the point. All employees who facilitate, or attend, meetings should be required to learn how to run, and be part of, a successful meeting.
- Requires every employee to utilize a time management system, formal or informal.
- Deals with its in-house nonstop talkers and time abusers. Gingerly at first, but deals with them nevertheless.
- Requires that telephones be picked up on the first ring, voice mail messages shortened, calls returned promptly.
- Respects visitors' time. From now on, "wait" should be considered a four-letter word.
- Encourages delegation. If we're not the best person for the job, we shouldn't be wasting our time doing it when someone else can do it faster. And better.
- Understands that this is the age of sound bites: shorter and quicker is better. Shorter and quicker applies to meetings, memos, letters, manuals, rules, and especially conversations, idle or otherwise.

Time management systems are like consultants. There are a million of them, all waiting anxiously to be picked out of the crowd. Before selecting the best one, however, we must first understand the depth of the problem and make the commitment to change.

Then it's time to study this subject of time management in detail and depth. (There is a wealth of information available at the library or the bookstore or the computer software store.) Only after we've done our homework can we pick from the many systems that exist and find the best one for us. (Don't worry, there's one out there for everybody.)

I am personally incapable of maintaining one of those industrial-strength time management systems that organizes everything from our trips to the bathroom to the time we spend with the kids. I admire those people who can make them work (do you need an engineering degree?), and I wish I were one. But I'm not.

It's enough for most of us, assuming we've made the unalterable commitment to improve our time management, to schedule our time on a daily and weekly basis, and then prioritize it, all the while making sure to respect the time of those around us. Write it down—a simple piece of paper is enough. Then, once we've got our own time under control, we can insist that those who work for us, and with us, do the same.

Think about it. What would our company be like if everybody were on time? If no one had to wait? How much additional work would each of us get done? How much time would we save? Five hours a week? Ten?

And what could every employee do with another five hours a week, 260 hours a year? What could our company do with those 260 hours a year, multiplied by the number of employees?

Scary, isn't it, the power we hold in our hands?

THE BOTTOM LINE

We don't condone people who steal our material possessions, why should we put up with those who steal our time?

Time lost is profit lost.

Time found is profit regained.

30

A Sense
of McUrgency

There is a magic word in sports. That word is "tempo" and it embraces every game I've ever played or seen. Tempo is everywhere in the games people play and it covers a multitude of strengths. And sins.

"I could never find the right tempo," the thrashing golfer wails.

"We played to their tempo, not to ours," the losing basketball coach moans.

"His tempo was faster than mine," the exhausted tennis player whines.

They're all talking about the same thing. Pace. As in the rate of activity. As in the ebb and the flow of the game.

Well, our business has a tempo, too. And its tempo is known as "sense of urgency," and it's established by the entrepreneur. It's the pace at which the business game is played.

If I were Webster I would define the phrase "sense of urgency" as follows:

Sense of urgency (colloq.) the pace of activity, almost always activated by concern.

"Pace of activity?"

To us business owners, our company's sense of urgency, or pace of activity, should begin at upbeat and ascend from there. Which means we should work on the balls of our feet and not on our heels. We should answer the phone on the first ring and not on the second, drop what we're doing when our customers call, and manage our time professionally. We should stop at the water cooler only when thirsty. Only long enough to quench our thirst.

"Activated by concern?"

This sense of urgency should be perpetuated by a cloud of concern hovering over all of our employees. A cloud of concern that our customers might not get what they want, when they want it. A cloud of concern that we might not achieve our personal and business goals by the end of the day. A cloud of concern that our quality might suffer, that our service might abate, and that our competitors might gain lost ground. This is a cultural cloud we're describing here, one that begins in our office and floats through every hallway, across every desk.

Just as the coach sets a basketball team's tempo, so we entrepreneurs define our business team's tempo. We are the cause of our employees' concern (or lack of concern), we give them a reason to care (or not to care), and we engender a sense of urgency (or a sense of lethargy).

And it is our employees' responsibility to adapt to our sense of urgency, whatever pace we decide to set. For, as always, we've hired them, and trained them, and promoted them. And could replace them.

This sense of urgency is real and tangible, and, like so many other corporate characteristics, can be immediately spotted. Visit a McDonald's during the lunch-hour rush. Stand back, observe the activity, the flurry of controlled motion. McDonald's employees have a pace of their own, a frenetic, controlled sense of urgency. You can see it and sense it and touch it, and it is fostered, no doubt, by a cloud of concern that is perpetuated from the corporate offices. A cloud of concern for McDonald's customers perhaps, or maybe for retaining each employee's job, or perhaps by a need for peer acceptance.

Whatever the cause, someone has created a visible sense of McUrgency in McDonald's employees. It is effective, and damned if their customers don't thrive on it. To the tune of a zillion or two burgers every year.

Our small business needs a sense of McUrgency too. And don't tell me it can't be done.

If McDonald's can do it from their far-off corporate offices, we can do it from right here.

THE BOTTOM LINE

Which will it be? A "sense of urgency" or a "turtle's pace"? That's for the entrepreneur to decide.

Every business has a tempo. Make yours upbeat.

31

It's the Little Things That Count

You don't have to be older than George Burns to remember the term "fringe benefits." I'm not and I do.

Well, the word "fringe" has all but disappeared from our business lexicon these days. Gone the way of the gray flannel suit.

For good reason, too. No benefits are fringe anymore. Everything counts, no matter how trivial, no matter how small.

Here's a list of some of those benefits that may appear small but count big. As in small cost, big payback.

Use one or use them all:

▪ Pick up the tab for employee education (night school or correspondence courses). The employee pays the upfront tuition, then is reimbursed later if the course is relevant and completed with a grade of C or better.

▪ Loan company equipment for off-hours use. Computers, trucks, office equipment, etc. (after making sure the insurance company agrees).

▪ Maintain an emergency loan fund. Say, up to two weeks' advance wages (for employees with a year or more of service). Noninterest bearing, payroll deduction payback, six months to repay.

▪ Be ready with an unwritten flex-hour policy for employees with onetime personal problems.

▪ Offer a phone-in counseling service for personal problems (substance abuse, marriage and family problems, etc.). A number of companies specialize in this kind of service. Ask your insurance carrier for names.

▪ Help employees resolve their individual problems with health insurance carriers. (The company's fist is always bigger.)

▪ Celebrate when the good news strikes. Little things, like doughnuts or pizza or lunchtime barbecues. And flip those burgers yourself.

▪ Most movie theaters offer corporate discount packets. Offer tickets to employees at the discounted rates. (And give them away randomly as rewards for attendance, quality achievements, difficult projects completed, etc.)

▪ Remember birthdays and anniversary dates. Send a card or post the occasion on the bulletin board or buy a cake. Celebrate together and mourn together. Teams are strengthened through shared concerns.

▪ Keep the restrooms spotless. I mean spotless. Nothing sends worse messages (to employees and to visitors) than unkempt restrooms.

▪ Keep windows clean, walls painted, parking lots swept, employee lunchrooms neat. Like home.

Why not? We spend almost as much time at the office. Maybe more.

▪ Have employees contribute to the newsletter. Thus it becomes a voice of the family, rather than a platform for the boss.

▪ Pick up the tab for a Christmas party and/or summer picnic. Establish a budget, ask for a volunteer planning committee, and turn the project over to it. (Suggestions and complaints will be directed to the committee, not to you.)

▪ Give sizable discounts on in-house products. No profits necessary on employee sales.

▪ Offer quit-smoking awards to those still afflicted. And pick up the tab for quit-smoking classes successfully completed.

▪ And finally, and this is a *must*, offer a 401(k) plan. It isn't expensive to administer, and there is no requirement that contributions must be matched. These plans are one of the last remaining tax shelters and they fill the role of a retirement plan as well.

All employees should have a 401(k) plan, whether they know it or not. And if they don't know it, it's up to us to educate them.

These are some of the little things that add up—to small businesses that say, "We care."

THE BOTTOM LINE

I The smallest deeds often send the biggest messages.   I

VII

The Making
of a Flexible
Manager

32

Who, Me?
A Focus Problem?

Who, me? A focus problem?

Well, I'm sorry, but I don't have a focus problem. Why, I can stand over a golf ball for less than ten seconds and focus on a half dozen thoughts. None of them related to golf.

See. I don't have a focus problem.

Unless, of course, I need to focus on whatever it is I'm doing, in which case I do have a focus problem. Especially if whatever I'm doing is something I don't enjoy. In which case, like I said, I do have a focus problem.

Hey, this issue of focus is not only a personal, everyday issue with most of us, it also applies to our business. And to our vision of our business. For instance, how many small businesses do you know that try to offer too many services? Or too many products? How many do you know that try to provide the best quality along with the fastest delivery as well as the lowest prices—all at the same time?

See what I mean? Just as we can't be all things to our company, so our company can't be all things to the marketplace. We need to focus on something.

The problem is, where focus is concerned, our small business resources are limited. Unlike Procter and Gamble or 3M, we don't have enough resources, either financial or human, to branch out in every direction. We don't have the resources to fund every idea. To pursue every vision.

Yes, our resources are finite, and they need to be invested in those activities that are likely to pay off. In those activities where we have a reasonable opportunity for success.

Nor should we be wasting our personal time or energy focusing on jobs or projects that someone else can do better. We mustn't be detoured from doing those things we do well, while overloading ourselves with those things we don't.

And the same thing is true of our company. If our company is weak in a product line or a service that isn't necessary to our mission, then we should dump it. The resources required for those unnecessary products or services will only dilute our available talent. Like the football coach, our job is to send the muscle where it does the most good.

Webster's defines *focus* as "to fix or settle on one thing; to concentrate." For business purposes we should expand that definition to include "the relentless pursuit of a project until it is completed in accordance with plan."

I hired my presidential replacement in the fall of 1989. It took the two of us an hour or so to identify and prioritize our ten biggest problems, and another few hours to outline a general plan by which to resolve all ten. So why do I need the guy? I wondered when we had finished. I could have done this alone.

It didn't take him long to open my eyes. I mean that man could focus. Of all the differences between him (a pedigreed professional manager) and me (a bona fide entrepreneur)—and there were many—the most noticeable was his ability to focus on whatever project he chose to pursue. Distractions that would pull me away from projects for days were only minor inconveniences to him. No matter how drab the project, once it got his attention, that project was going to get done. You could bet your to-do list on it. Nothing stood in his way.

Not so with most entrepreneurs. Give us a choice between solving an order entry problem and satisfying a customer and guess which one gets done? Adios, order entry problem.

Following is a collection of tips on the subject of focus. All learned the hard way:

1. If a project is important enough to begin, it is important enough to conclude.

2. Learn to intensify your attention, from meetings to one-on-one discussions. Block out diversions. Say no to interruptions. Bear down.

3. Make the right choices up front. Learn to limit your activities to those you are capable of achieving and those you have ample time to finish.

4. Just as you prioritize your time each day, so you should prioritize your long-term and short-term projects. And all should remain on your to-do list until completed.

5. Learn how to prioritize as well as how to say no. An overflowing plate is the enemy of focus. You don't have to be all things to all people, that's why you hire superstars. Delegate, but don't overload.

6. When one project must give way to another, make sure the first is temporarily concluded at a convenient spot. Then adopt a steadfast plan for its resumption.

7. There is a correlation between *interest* and *focus*. While interest can, in the short term, become an incentive through motivation, it is difficult to maintain for long periods of time. Don't expect to focus for long periods of time on subjects that don't interest you.

8. Any problem-solving exercise involves three steps: identifying the issue, planning its resolution, and focusing on the solution. Without focus the first two are wasted.

9. Focus, and the lack thereof, is a cultural issue. If the entrepreneur doesn't finish the projects he begins, his employees won't either. And a team specializing in half-finished projects is a half-finished team.

The professional managers of this world know that the ability to focus pays dividends. They have learned that it is far better to solve one problem forever than to have three in various stages of irresolution.

THE BOTTOM LINE

Concentrated focus creates excellence. Diluted focus begets mediocrity.

Too much too soon is the enemy of focus. Attack problems and opportunities one step at a time.

Focus requires patience, attention to detail, concentration, an organized and adhered-to agenda, and a dogged attention span over long periods of time. Entrepreneurs' nightmares, all.

33

Don't Try
to Run Marathons
Alone

Why bother writing a chapter on delegation, right? I mean, what kind of idiot do I think I'm writing to, the guy who invented workers' comp? Why, of course every entrepreneur understands the importance of delegation. It's so obvious.

Well, if it's so obvious, why don't we do more of it?

Because we're entrepreneurs, that's why. Because doing things ourselves got us where we are today. Because doing things ourselves is easier. And faster. Wastes less motion. Less time.

But we're trying to make a change in the way we lead people, aren't we? We're trying to make the transition from entrepreneur to manager, aren't we? We're trying to leverage our talents and our skills, aren't we?

OK, so what's the big deal about delegating, anyway? Why can't we do whatever it is ourselves?

Because entrepreneurs are sprinters, and managers are marathoners and the long-term success of our business is a long-distance race. Thus we need the legs of our employees to help us run those marathons that sprinters can't finish.

Which means that it's imperative that we learn how to delegate. That we learn to hand the baton to someone who is capable of running the distances, who can help us reach the finish line. Because without that someone we're destined to run the race alone, which means we'll hit the wall somewhere around the ten-mile mark. (Look it up. This is exactly what happens to 60 percent of all small-business start-ups sometime within the first five years.)

And that baton gives us leverage, because a manager's output (and we're managers now, remember?) is not what comes or goes from his desk, it's what comes or goes from his department. Or his team. Or, in our case, our output is what comes or goes from our company.

Oh yes, and this process of delegating is not to be confused with the process of dumping. If our employee perceives that he's being dumped on, we've probably delegated the task but not the authority. It's all in the way that we delegate.

Sure, I know there's an element of risk in delegating authority, but if we don't feel comfortable with that risk, then we've probably done the delegating to the wrong person. And if we don't have the right person to delegate to, then it's time to turn back to the chapter on hiring.

It should be understood that along with the passing of the baton comes more than increased expectations. Acceptance of the baton also denotes the granting of trust, at the same time that it shifts responsibility.

From that point on it's the responsibility of whoever was handed the baton to win the race. Or to lose it.

Here's a collection of tips on how to pass the baton:

1. Remember that the ultimate goal of delegation is not to get rid of the work. Nor is it to keep employees busy. The ultimate goal is to increase the output of the department, team, or company.

2. Don't delegate the method, delegate the task. Let the person you delegate to determine the method.

3. Make sure that the person you delegate to buys in to the task, agrees to the time frame, and accepts the responsibility. (If you're unwilling to delegate the responsibility, don't bother delegating the task.)

4. Make sure the person you delegate to has input into what constitutes accomplishment. Goals should be measurable.

5. Once the task is assigned, keep your distance. It's OK to ask for updates, but don't snoop or pry. (If you feel you must, you've delegated to the wrong person.)

6. Avoid excessive reporting.

7. Follow up only on target dates, or when the project is finished. (Or when it should be finished.)

8. Make the person delegated to accountable for his success or failure. Reward success, punish failure.

9. Beware of overdelegation to superstars. If you find you're relying too heavily on one employee, then you have a superstar shortage. (And you're about to have a bigger superstar shortage if you don't balance the overloaded superstar's workload.)

And finally, do not confuse the delegatee with the gofer.
Gofers go fer because they got to.
Delegatees go fer because they want to.

THE BOTTOM LINE

From delegation comes leverage, the key to personal growth.
  Trust is the basis for effective delegation. If you don't trust, then you can't delegate.

34

How Can We Resolve It When We Don't Want to Face It?

Every organization, from small business to Fortune 500, includes a collection of imperfect human beings presided over by an imperfect leader. No organization is exempt, ours included.

Given that imperfection, what is sure to evolve?

Why, conflict, of course. Conflict between us and our employees. Conflict between our employees and themselves. And conflict between us and outsiders, and between our employees and outsiders. More conflict than we could ever imagine, and every speck of it screaming to be resolved.

Those of us who are hardened conflict-avoiders are doomed to managerial failure if we don't learn how to face that conflict. And resolve it. Because unresolved conflict only results in more unresolved conflict. And as that unresolved conflict festers and escalates, the stakes only get higher. And higher.

Years ago, I had an art director who showed up in the morning on his time, not mine. And his day began approximately one hour after mine. And everyone else's. The guy was creative, productive, and earned every penny of his paycheck. But my 8:00 A.M. rules were for the rest of the team. Not for him.

Soon the entire art department was up to his tricks. Cocky about it, too. And before long I had five people sauntering in between 8:30 and 9:00 instead of one.

And now I had a much bigger problem on my hands. An entire art department on the art director's in-your-face flexible hours. (Just try to change the behavior of five artists sometime. I dare you.) The result was that six months later we had a brand-spanking-new art department. Art director and all.

An expensive price to pay for my initial aversion to conflict, wouldn't you say? Had I dealt with the art director's tardiness at the beginning, that cleansing might never have occurred.

Don't look now, but here are some of the subtle messages we send when we avoid conflict:

- We don't give a damn. Rules are made to be broken. It's OK to come to work late. It's OK to come up short on goals. It's OK to underachieve.
- We won't deal with problems, conflictive or otherwise. (Who wants to work for leaders who won't solve problems?)
- We play favorites. (In my case, the art department.) Let the backbiting begin.
- We can be manipulated. By our employees, our customers, our vendors, our neighbor's dog.
- We have an IQ deficiency.

Everyone knows that the more people we manage, the more conflict we must face. It's a function of growth and human nature. We don't belong at the helm of our company if we can't understand that. And do something about it.

Conflict isn't a tonic for most folks (although I do know a few who enjoy it), but the results of dealing with it are usually positive, when it's resolved professionally. I'm reminded of the conflict that resulted from salary negotiations with the man I hired to replace me as president.

The interviews had gone well (for both of us). It was time to get down to dollars and cents.

He got tough and conflictive. I got angry and irrational.

But I finally cooled off and he eventually eased up and we worked things out. And when all was said and done he had achieved most of his goals and I had achieved most of mine. And he got the salary he was looking for and I got the tough and wily negotiator I was looking for. A fellow who, unlike me, had no problem conflicting. As a matter of fact, I think he rather enjoyed it.

So once we've determined that conflict is worth facing, what's the next step?

Resolve it, of course. One on one. Face to face. Eyeball to eyeball, trading today's unpleasantries for tomorrow's improvements.

Here's a true story with a conflict-resolving punch line that works every time. The moral, I'll tip you in advance, is that when two people are high-power conflicting, their biggest barrier to resolution is listening. Or lack of it.

The story goes like this:

John is on my right, Barbara on my left, both coiled to strike. We're in a Denver motel room hunched over a table, its tabletop chipped at the corners. If glares were lethal, I'd be the only survivor.

Barbara, hardheaded production manager, and John, superstar salesman with ego to match, were back in the trenches again. Their frequent skirmishes, ongoing for months, had escalated into war.

Me to the rescue. Good old nonconflictive me. (Grasping at straws, I'd read a magazine article on conflict resolution on the plane ride to Denver.)

"Well," I open semiconfidently, turning to Barbara. "We seem to have a communication breakdown here. What's the problem?"

She straightens her shoulders and rubs her hands, preparing to attack. A crooked smile brushes her lips as John stiffens, his breathing labored.

"John," I remind him, following the magazine's script. "When

Barbara's finished, I want you to paraphrase for me exactly what she said."

John cocks his head and frowns, the rebuttals formed and waiting on his pursed lips. This wasn't a part of his plan. I can hear his gears grinding. Listen? How can I listen and argue at the same time?

Frowning, John pulls out paper and pen as Barbara's smile widens.

And then it's *whoooosh* as Barbara unloads. Disarmed, defenseless, and forced to be attentive, John listens, glowers, and writes. When she's finished, he paraphrases the highlights, and lowlights, of the words he's just heard. Barbara looks on, vindicated.

And now it's John's turn. He warms to the task and soon his face is a splotchy red. Barbara listens, scribbling frantically. Finally, out of breath, John finishes. Dazed, Barbara repeats his list of atrocities. Only then do I detect a sign of victory, as John's forehead furrows while Barbara nods resignedly.

John peers at his notes, then turns to me, blushing ever so slightly. Barbara rolls her eyes. They've listened. They know.

Not exactly the Treaty of Paris, I say to myself, but we have a beginning. A place to start. We talk on into the afternoon and the sneers turn into reluctant negotiation and finally into resolution.

Damned if this listening stuff doesn't work, I think to myself. Where's it been all these years?

Here's a collection of tips on how to resolve conflict:

1. Never dive into conflict on the spur of the moment, especially the high-powered stuff. Mull it over, think it through, always consider the downsides. Then prepare for the confrontation as you would for an important meeting, because that's exactly what it is.

2. State your purpose at the outset of the confrontation. Keep personalities out of it. (The purpose of any confrontation should be "to improve the working environment," or "to increase efficiency,"

or "to improve the product." Not to change John's or Barbara's or anyone's behavior.)

3. Hear all parties out. Give everyone a chance to vent.

4. Ask the conflictees to recommend a solution. Then negotiate.

5. Offer alternatives. Then negotiate some more.

6. Agree on a course of action.

7. Set a target date for correction.

8. Be businesslike. Don't play God, do control your emotions, do avoid threats.

9. There are three possible results when conflict is resolved: (1) we win, (2) they win, and (3) everybody wins (win-win). Number 3 should always be the objective.

Win-win comes only from compromise, never from dictating. In all honest and fair negotiations no one party ever completely wins, but all parties should be able to walk away from the conflict feeling that the outcome was the best for the team.

10. Keep the resolution confidential (unless agreed otherwise), between the participants involved.

Conflict in a diverse working environment is inevitable. As a matter of fact, conflict in any working environment is inevitable, diverse or otherwise. We had better learn how to face it and resolve it.

Or find someone who can.

THE BOTTOM LINE

Conflict resolved results in improvement. Conflict avoided results in escalated conflict.

The wielding of power will not resolve conflict. It will only postpone it. Only negotiation resolves conflict.

Face conflict head on. The meek may inherit the earth, but they will never qualify for the Managers' Hall of Fame.

35

Now Hear This!

We all have gaps in our knowledge base. You know what I mean. There are certain things our brains can't handle. Things we'll never understand.

What's yours? Advanced calculus? Nuclear fission? *Saturday Night Live*?

Me? Mine was always Hubert Humphrey. I never could understand that guy.

No, I'm not saying I could never understand what he said. What I mean is I could never understand how he could violate an iron-clad, immutable law of the universe every waking minute of every day and still rise to the head of his class.

What ironclad, immutable law am I referring to? Why, the law of talking and listening, that's what law I'm talking about. (You know, the law that says that people cannot talk and listen at the same time.)

Not so with old Hubert. He was the only person I've ever seen who could do both simultaneously without batting an eyelash. The rest of us mere mortals fall into the one-organ-at-a-time category. Which is to say, if our mouths are moving, our ears must be taking a break. And vice versa.

But keeping one's mouth moving is only one of the many activities that work against effective listening. There are a host of others, including:

- Predicting what the speaker will say next
- Thinking of a response before the speaker is finished
- Distorting what we hear due to personal bias
- Allowing ourselves to be distracted by a thought, or by an outside influence
- Evaluating the message before we understand it
- Reacting emotionally to specific words or positions

Put all of these barriers to good listening together and what do we have? The undeniable fact that the art of listening is a lot harder to master than the reflex of talking. Is it any wonder that most of us do a lot more of the latter than the former?

Here's what should be done to make better listeners of us all: instead of being required to attend high school or college we should all have to be salespeople for two years (straight commission, of course). Make our living peddling doodads of one sort or another before drifting off to become doctors or lawyers or Indian chiefs.

Why? Because if salespeople don't listen, then they don't sell. Period. That's because today's customers demand to be heard, and if the salesperson in front of them doesn't listen, they'll go find another one who will. And when that happens the nonlistening salesperson won't have any money left over to buy groceries or beer. And then he'll either starve to death or die of boredom, whichever comes first.

See what I mean? You'd learn to listen, too.

Here's a collection of tips on how to become an effective listener:

1. Listen to understand, not to reply.

2. For better understanding, try to put yourself in the speaker's shoes.

3. When possible, prepare to listen. Review relevant material in advance of a planned listening situation (a meeting, interview, sales call). Set listening goals. Have an overriding purpose for listening (to solve a problem, to learn, to sell a widget).

4. Learn to paraphrase, both mentally and on paper. Summarize main ideas, key words, and phrases.

5. Write it down. Never be caught in an important listening situation without paper and pencil.

6. Don't jump to conclusions. Control your emotions. Remember, the speaker may only need to vent. Who knows, the act of venting alone may solve his problems.

7. Take time out to think. Understand that silence is OK. It's tough to say something that's offensive to others when your lip is zipped.

What's more, the person who speaks infrequently is more apt to be heard than the person who rattles on incessantly.

8. Recognize that conflict is often necessary to the process of successful listening. The listener's goal should not be to avoid conflict, but rather to resolve the problem that's behind it.

9. Give the speaker adequate feedback. Respond in a way that lets him know his message is being received.

10. Summarize verbally when finished. Let the speaker know you heard what was said.

11. Learn to look for body language. It's always more definitive than words.

12. And when in doubt as to whom to listen to, go to the source. The people with the answers, the people who really know. Like customers and line workers and telephone operators.

Not the folks in the middle. Go to those at the end. Or to those at the beginning.

And don't forget that listening doesn't involve only the ears. The brain, the heart, and the eyes should take part, too.

Like when you hear your neighbor's Doberman barking at night. Be sure to engage the brain before you act.

Or when Little Orphan Annie bounces her rent check. Be sure to engage the heart before you call the sheriff.

Or when Lizzie Borden tells you she loves you. Be sure to engage the eyes before you rewrite your will.

See what I mean?

Good listening. It's a sum of the senses.

THE BOTTOM LINE

Too often the mouth is quicker than the ears. Learn to reverse the process.

Listening never creates problems, it only resolves them.

36

How to Upside
a Downside

My company grew relentlessly between 1985 and 1990. Five rapid-fire years of 30 percent sales growth, sometimes more. An entrepreneur's fairy tale. A dream come true. Peaches and cream.

Peaches and cream, hell, try fire and brimstone. Hell and high water. Hairballs and sludge.

Now don't misunderstand me; I had planned carefully for that growth. Well, the upsides of it anyway. I had considered every last detail of those things about a growing business that I enjoyed. Things like arranging new facilities, purchasing new equipment, assembling new team members.

And the downsides? Sorry, but what entrepreneur worth his rose-colored glasses worries about planning for downsides? Not me. And, make no mistake about it, five consecutive years of 30 percent growth brings deluges, no, make that tidal waves, of opportunities for downsides, capable of engulfing everything in their path. Nothing escapes those tidal waves, from management to vendors to systems and controls. All the way down to the balance sheet.

Sure, I could have planned for those downsides had I envisioned them. But downsides and roadblocks aren't what entrepreneurs are all about. We're all about upsides and opportunities. And if we don't have someone to rattle our cage when the downside warnings begin to appear, they'll do to us what our competitors never could.

Where do those entrepreneurial downsides come from, you ask? From everywhere, brother, and I do mean from everywhere. From sources like:

1. Too much growth. Thirty percent sales growth requires 30 percent management improvement. As well as 30 percent systems improvement and 30 percent controls improvement, even as they put 30 percent more strain on the creaking balance sheet. Try a steady diet of this for five years and watch a few fires go out. Including your own.

2. Too little growth. Grow or die, someone once said, and it applies to business and life as well as to flowers and weeds. You see that axiom at work every day in the computer, airline, and defense industries. Eventually it will happen to your industry too, if you're around long enough.

3. Government policies. Taxes, health care reform, red tape, bureaucracy, tariffs, duties, treaties, OSHA, regulations, glurg, glurg . . .

4. Competitors. God bless their price-cutting, innovative, take-no-prisoner souls.

5. New technology. Products (or services) come and products (or services) go. Nothing is sacred in the business of doing business, nothing is forever. Ask IBM shareholders if you have any doubts on this one.

6. Random events. Interest rates, and the economy, and hurricanes and floods and earthquakes and droughts and sickness and pestilence and retirement and . . .

Discouraging, wouldn't you agree?

But downsides don't have to be fatalsides. Or even criticalsides. Or serioussides. They can even turn into upsides if we arm our team thoroughly and are prepared to meet them head on. And upsides beget opportunities and opportunities beget growth and growth's what entrepreneurs are here for, isn't it?

Here's what it takes to upside a downside:

1. An entrepreneur at the helm who anticipates downsides. Or, more likely, an entrepreneur at the helm who will listen to someone else who anticipates downsides.

2. Planning, planning, and more planning.

Planning is the natural enemy of downsides. Planning means devising a defense, and building an offense, and marshaling the troops. Managerial duties, all three.

3. A lean machine in the first place. Lean in those sensitive and fragile areas where danger always lurks. Areas like quality control and inventory and waterfalls in the lobby.

4. Diversification. Don't put all of your eggs in one basket, and don't give all of your baskets to one bunny. Spread responsibility and the opportunity for success around.

5. Training. Educating your employees (as well as yourself) in the ways of those downsides. And preparing the team to react when the downsides strike.

And remember, it's our employees who do the planning, and take part in the training, and create that lean machine of ours. And if we don't have capable ones in all the right places, the downsides will take care of themselves.

Whether we anticipate them or not.

THE BOTTOM LINE

Downsides are inevitable. But fatal, or even serious, downsides aren't.

Some entrepreneurs are incapable of foreseeing downsides. In which case, hire a devil's advocate. Then heed him.

37

Beware of the Fad-of-the-Month Club

There's nothing new in the world of small business. Everything that is happening today has happened before—someone's organization has needed restructuring, someone's employees have needed motivating, someone's culture has needed changing.

So what are we poor entrepreneurs to do, when we think it's time for a dose of something new in our business? What system should we use, whose advice should we take, which of the latest fads should we embrace?

If you're like me you glom onto the latest book, attend the trendiest seminar, or hire the loudest consultant. Maybe all three. And you become a member of the Fad-of-the-Month Club.

Then you engross yourself in participative management, or turn your organization chart upside down, or opt for employee ownership, or job enrichment, or shower a deluge of human resource goodies on your employees. And if you can't determine which of the above to do, just keep your eyes open. There'll be something new along shortly.

The truth of the matter is there isn't just *one* thing that will turn our company around. And there isn't just *one* thing that will change our culture, or correct our infrastructure, or unite our employees. Just as there isn't *one* thing that wins football games. Or cures heart disease. Or corrupts politicians.

Here is a partial list of those once-in-a-lifetime cure-alls that appear every year or so, except that they really aren't once-in-a-lifetime, they're once-every-few-months, and they really aren't cure-alls, they're only incremental aids:

1. Participative management. Great in theory, and it can work wonders when organized carefully and phased in over long periods of time. But don't give away the keys to the vault too soon. After all, the typical entry-level, hourly entrepreneurial employee is young, inexperienced, and too often transitory, and we aren't exactly Lee Iacocca or Jack Welch when it comes to exhibiting management skills. Besides, not all employees are cut out to make key decisions, even if they want to.

Embrace participative management, but embrace it gingerly and phase it in slowly, over a long period of time. And don't expect miracles, especially in the short term.

2. Expensive human resource packages. Sure, high wages and gracious benefits win popularity contests, but only in the year in which they are granted. After that they become employee rights. Try cutting your health insurance program in half or giving the ax to the annual Christmas bonus if you don't believe me.

3. Job enrichment. One person's enrichment is another's entombment. Some employees like the way things are, and they don't want any more responsibility than they already have. These employees prefer to be left alone.

As with participative management, the employees must be right or job enrichment won't work. (Which puts us back on the subject of hiring again.)

4. The nice guy management syndrome. We might want to be perceived as kind and gracious as old St. Nick, but the difference is

we don't have elves and reindeer on our payroll. We do have employees on our payroll and they don't always respond like elves and reindeer. And elves and reindeer don't win or lose in the game of capitalism, anyway. Motivated and productive employees win or lose.

5. Employee ownership. Sharing the pie isn't as easy as it sounds. Sometimes there isn't enough pie to go around, and sometimes the pie isn't divided the way everyone would like it to be, and sometimes our employees would rather bet their future on T-bills, anyway.

Oh yes, and all of the time minority shareholders, especially those who double as employees, can be a pain in the neck.

So what does all this mean?

It means there is no quick correction, no easy cure, no fail-safe solution to resolving our management problems. It means we shouldn't go nuts on the latest behavioral-science fad until we've explored its downsides. Until we're aware of its costs.

How will we know for sure?

We'll never be sure until we've tried every fad, but we can give the latest one the test it deserves. Tests like:

- Networking other companies that have tried it already. (Don't be the first to jump in—the downsides are too dangerous.)
- Assigning investigatory committees.
- Taking employee polls.
- Walking the production floor. Asking questions.
- Reading, consulting, and listening.
- And above all, not moving too quickly. Diagnose the hell out of the options. (Once adopted, fads are expensive to drop, and once dropped, fads destroy management's credibility.)

And one final thought on the subject of guiding our company. You don't have to be terminally ill before you call in the doctor.

Check the thermometer once in a while, whether you think your patient is healthy or not. X-ray it and see for yourself what's going on inside.

And whatever you do, be careful of the latest fad, but be mindful of it, too. Pet rocks and Volkswagen Beetles were fads not so long ago. So were faxes and pizza.

THE BOTTOM LINE

From impulsiveness come hangovers and regrets. Proceed slowly.

Beware of the latest fad, yet be aware of it, too.

38

It's the Message We Send

How many times has this happened to you?

It's annual performance review time. One of your employees (who also doubles as a friend and a superstar) fidgets nervously on the far side of your desk. You begin the review (following the script) with a complimentary remark, then dive into the guts of the presentation.

Your intent? To improve performance.

Ten minutes later your employee, friend, and resident superstar storms out of your office, slamming the door behind him.

What happened? He perceived you were attacking him personally.

Or how about this?

It's employee meeting time. You're briefing the troops on the new 401(k) plan options.

"Any questions?" you ask.

"Why don't you pay 100 percent of our health care like Megabig Corporation does?" one of your employees asks.

You rant and rave and fume for five minutes, then storm out of the meeting, slamming the door behind you. What happened? You perceived the guy was attacking you and the way you run your business.

And that's how perception works. Facts and intent don't mean diddly-squat. It's only perception that counts. And it works that way in so many real-life situations as well. For example:

. . . it matters not whether President Clinton is doing the job the right way. If the voters *perceive* he's doing it the wrong way, it's back to Arkansas for him.

. . . and it matters not whether Keating screwed all those bond holders on purpose. The jury *perceived* he did and they put the sumbitch on ice.

. . . and it matters not whether Frank thinks he's the friendliest, mellowest soul in the office. If his coworkers *perceive* him to be a surly psychopath, then he is a surly psychopath.

. . . and it matters not whether we see ourselves as a wonderful employer and a visionary leader. If our employees *perceive* us to be a lecherous worm and a money-grubbing cad, then by God, we are a lecherous worm and a money-grubbing cad.

So what, you ask?

1. So remember when leading people (as entrepreneurs and CEOs and presidents are supposed to do), it matters not what you think or believe. All that matters is what your employees perceive you think or believe. If they perceive you don't give a hoot about their problems, then they don't give a hoot about your problems. If they perceive the pursuit of quality is not important to you, then the pursuit of quality is not important to them. If they perceive you think the customer is a pain in the posterior, then the customer is a pain in their posterior.

And once your employees don't think your company and your customers and your quality are important, you have a serious cultural problem. One that takes years of leadership to set straight.

2. When trying to change employee behavior, remember you're dealing with the way you perceive them, not with what they believe

or the way they think. Most employees can deal with this concept of perception—its not like their beliefs are being challenged or their thinking is being attacked.

3. Ditto when communicating with employees about the decisions you've made or the leadership you've provided. They aren't attacking you personally, they're only doing what comes naturally. Trying to improve their life.

4. Presentation is everything. Employee review? Shareholder meeting? Wedding proposal? It matters not what you intend to communicate, it's the way your presentation is perceived that counts. Prepare with care, taking pains to hear your words through a listener's ear.

Try this. Try asking a collection of employees (allow anonymity, of course) how you, and your company, are perceived. Ask them for a one-to-ten rating on whatever you deem important to the success of your business. They can be cultural issues, management issues, or leadership traits—and can run the gamut from ethics, respect for the individual, customer responsiveness, and systems to trust, follow-up, accountability, and focus. Whatever perception you want to measure.

Then compare their rating to yours. Does their perception agree with yours?

My guess? It isn't even close.

Like it or not, when it comes to dealing with people, or being dealt with by people, facts matter hardly at all. It's only perception that counts.

THE BOTTOM LINE

It isn't what we think or believe. It's only the message we send.
It isn't truth that makes followers follow. It's their perception of truth.

VIII

Getting the Most
Out of the Entrepreneur

39

Ask Questions First

Here's a hypothetical question for you.

Let's pretend your best customer has just dropped the ultimate bomb. Closed his account and marched off to a competitor.

What's the first thing you should do?

1. Raise holy hell and fire the salesperson.
2. Raise holy hell and fire the sales manager.
3. Raise holy hell and put out a contract on the customer.
4. Ask questions first. Ask the salesperson and the sales manager and the customer a series of open-ended questions.

Of course the correct answer is D. Ask questions first. Open-ended questions.

And maybe you'll learn why the customer hit the road before you burn any bridges. And maybe you'll get him back. And even if you don't, you're bound to learn something from the answers to your questions. And prevent other customers from dropping their bombs.

And *then* you raise holy hell.

History would be entirely different if this "ask questions first" technique had been employed by our ancestors. Relatives of General Custer would dot South Dakota today, the Alamo would be just another rickety old church, and Abe Lincoln would have seen the rest of the play.

This Case of the Departing Customer isn't the only time this open-ended question routine can be employed. Consider, for instance:

"Harry, your sales have been under projections for six months in a row. What can we do to reverse this trend?"

Or:

"Lillith, six invoices went out wrong last week. How can we make sure that doesn't happen again?"

Or:

"Frank, you walk in the office at 8:15 while everybody else arrives at 8:00. How can I explain this to the rest of my employees?"

What's about to happen here, whether it's Frank, Lillith, or Harry, is that the first stage of the negotiation process is about to begin. You and Frank, or Lillith, or Harry, are about to negotiate a solution to the problem du jour. And what better way to open those negotiations than to let the other person make the opening offer?

And here's another way to use the "ask questions first" routine:

Your sales manager roars into your office and plops down in a chair. "Production's done it again," he moans. "Acme's order went out late."

"Oh no," you commiserate, shaking your head. "What would you do with the production department if you were me?"

And then what happens?

Maybe he pulls out a machine gun and threatens a top-to-bottom restructuring of the production department, but more likely he gathers his wits about him and considers your question. And maybe he comes up with a workable solution.

Or maybe you gather your wits about you while he is considering your question. And you come up with a workable solution.

Or maybe you gather your wits about you and he gathers his wits about him and the two of you come up with a workable solution. And that's how it works. Ask questions first. Then let the other person do the talking and the venting and the thinking while you do the asking and the listening and the thinking.

The solution won't be far behind.

THE BOTTOM LINE

| When in doubt, don't spout. Ask. |

40

Sleep on It

The worst decisions are made at the most emotional times.

I should know.

I should never have kicked our number one vendor off our key supplier list after his late delivery cost us a sizable order. And I should never have slammed down the phone on that Chicago lawyer, even though he deserved it. And I should never have hired that mediocre CFO, even though I had been three lonely weeks without one. Each of those decisions, made in anger and desperation, eventually came back to haunt me.

I wish I had known then what I know now. *The worst decisions are made at the most emotional times.*

And the converse is just as true. *The best decisions are made when the head is the clearest.*

You have a tough decision to make? A game-breaking decision? Think it over. Take it slow. Do your research. Ask your questions. Solicit opinions. Consider alternatives.

Then go home. Sleep on it. The answer will come.

That's how the best decisions are made.

Following are the rules the president of the United States

follows when he has an important decision to make (they also apply to the president of General Motors and the president of Acme Laundry and Drycleaning as well):

- Be steady. (That's what Americans most want from their president, and what adversaries most respect.)
- Don't get captured by the event. (History is full of presidents who have been obsessed with a crisis or an impending decision.)
- Don't act until you must. (Rash decisions based on emotion and insufficient information are the biggest dangers in a crisis.)
- Talk, talk, talk. Think, think, think. Negotiate, negotiate, negotiate. (Use the telephone to take charge and coordinate strategy with other heads of state.)

The underlying strategy here for all presidents, large and small? Keep cool. Stay in control. Allow plenty of time to reach a decision. Wait until your emotions are subdued.

Personally, I'm glad I have an active set of emotional glands. Or whatever it is that secretes that stuff that makes one feel good. Or bad. No, I'm not ashamed of the fact: my emotions have a wide range of associated benefits. And they certainly don't make me a bad person.

But they sure can make me a lousy manager, unless I learn to control them.

Emotions are like teenagers—difficult to control, impossible to orchestrate. Plus, they go only one way—their way. And once they begin their relentless charge, the rush clogs our arteries, consumes our brain, and clouds everything we do. Our logic, our experience, our sense of what's best for our vision is thrown to the wind, a leaf in a November gale.

Whether we like it or not, the biggest decisions, in life and in business, usually come only once. Rarely are we allowed a second chance.

"I'll get back to you tomorrow," are the words for those make-it-or-break-it times.

Then go home. Have a beer. Go for a ride with the kids. And sleep on it.

THE BOTTOM LINE

Take your time. Stretch it, borrow it, buy more of it, do whatever it takes to avoid emotion-clouded decisions.

Decisions made are etched commitments. Decisions postponed are lingering opportunities.

41

The Shoe on
the Other Foot

I have a friend who went from the pits to the parapets overnight. One day he was a member of the masses, the next he was overseeing the masses. Lost in the shuffle on Friday, he was the dealer of the deck on Monday.

Suddenly he went from being one of two hundred partners to become president of his company.

And then management wasn't "them" anymore, management was "us." And then there wasn't someone else to blame, there was only himself. And then his company wasn't on the brink of hellfire and damnation anymore, it was on the brink of sunshine and survival.

Ah, the eyes of the beholder. What a difference perspective makes.

It was strange watching this sudden change in my friend's perspective. Nothing (other than the organization chart) had really changed. His company still sold the same products, still pursued the same customers, still plied the same industry. Nor had any of their key employees changed. Yet my friend's outlook went from Republican to Democrat in the snap of a finger. From hawk to dove. From employee to employer.

Not because of any earthshaking competitive event, mind you. No siree, it was his perspective alone that had changed. He had donned a new pair of shoes.

Let's face it, in politics, in management, and in anything else that deals with people, nothing is black and white. Nothing is right or wrong. Everything is one shade of gray or another. And that shade depends on the beholder's perspective.

So how did this change in perspective affect the way my friend performed his day-to-day duties?

1. Suddenly he had to learn how to shift perspective in the midst of a crisis. From employee to employer. From one employee to another. From customer to vendor back to customer again. Just long enough to understand. Just long enough to care.

2. All points of view (not just those from his own turf) had to be considered when making the tough decisions.

3. Gray suddenly became a synonym for flexible, where people and decision making were concerned.

4. In general, his gray decisions had to favor the team, however unpopular they might have been with individuals or small groups. (While gray decisions may affect the working conditions and job functions of employees, they must never infringe on their rights.)

5. Communications and presentation suddenly became important. He had to go to extraordinary lengths to communicate his gray decisions, in terms that all employees could understand and accept, even when they didn't agree.

Where my friend had been questioning and suspicious of management before, suddenly his mood changed to one of compassion and understanding. He recognized that effective management requires ample doses of both. (He has since learned that it is impossible to resolve an issue equitably without the aid of compassion and understanding.)

And so it is. The Middle East, the shipping department, the laggard CFO—the issue makes little difference. There is a solution to every problem, and that solution always requires an application of compassion and understanding.

There's a bonus, incidentally, that comes from managing with compassion and understanding. It's called leadership, and it's reserved for those who have learned to take off their shoes long enough to slip into someone else's.

Note how history's great generals made the rounds of the trenches. They slept there and they ate there, swallowing the infantry's dust. Not because they needed the exposure to frontline danger, but because they needed exposure to their soldiers' perspective.

Well, the same thing applies to today's successful managers. They aren't the ones with the best education and the most degrees. They are the managers, people like my friend, who have come to understand what it is that makes their number one asset tick. People who have arrived at that understanding by having been in opposing shoes before. If not in deed, at least in perspective.

Today, as the rights and the needs of the individual gain momentum with every court ruling, this issue of perspective is no longer an advantage in dealing with employees. It's a necessity.

The best thing about perspective? It isn't elusive. We don't have to make wrenching behavioral or intellectual changes to achieve it. We don't have to become a college professor or a priest to grasp its true meaning.

Which is to say, we don't have to drive a truck to understand truck drivers. What we do have to do is learn how to peer through their eyes. Borrowed eyes. Temporary eyes. Eyes without prejudice. Eyes that eschew snap judgments. Eyes that don't make assumptions until all viewpoints are considered.

This isn't an intellectual issue we're talking here. Nor an emotional one. It's common sense. A sidestep, a detour, a slight alteration.

A simple change of shoes.

THE BOTTOM LINE

Never judge an employee until you've stood in his place.
The eyes of the beholder may provide the answer, but it's the
shoes of the beholder that afford the opportunity.

42

Don't Be
Afraid to . . .

Don't Be Afraid to
Say You Were Wrong

Question: What do you think happens when we screw up in front of our employees and then pull the old Richard Nixon stonewall routine? Do our employees recognize our screwup? How about our denial?

And do they then shrug it off? Or do they broadcast the news, sniggering and giggling behind our backs?

Answer: Darn right they recognize our screwups. (Just as we recognize theirs.) And of course they resent our reluctance to admit our mistakes. (Just as we resent their reluctance to admit theirs.)

And no, they don't shrug it off, they broadcast the news to whoever is willing to listen, but they won't snigger and giggle, they'll guffaw and jeer. Until the last vestiges of our credibility are gone. And our image gets clobbered again.

How can they know when we screw up?

How can they not know? Unless, of course, we've assembled a team of stumblebums and bozos, in which case it won't make any difference.

So what's the big deal about admitting mistakes anyway? After all, we're not politicians; we don't depend on someone's vote to hold our job. And besides, mistakes aren't that big a deal. Our corporate culture allows them, doesn't it? And everybody is allowed to make them, aren't they? And we're as liable to make them as anyone else, aren't we? (Nowhere is it written that entrepreneurs can't make mistakes. The truth is, we probably make more than the average man on the street. Mistakes are our birthright; they come with the entrepreneurial turf.)

So lighten up, folks, and fess up when you screw up. And hold on for dear life to your credibility; it's the most valuable leadership trait you own.

Don't Be Afraid to Say You Don't Know

What's wrong with not having all the answers? After all, who do we know who does have them all, except for maybe our kids and H. Ross Perot?

What are our choices when we don't know?

Our choices are two. We can either say, "I don't know," in which case we'll be provided with the answer by someone who does. Or we can b.s. our way through the question, in which case we'll remain in the dark forever.

Now I ask you, what kind of choice is that?

Come on, admit it. It's not only acceptable to say, "I don't know," when we don't know, it's preferable. It isn't a sign of weakness, you know, it's a sign of honesty. And humility.

And speaking of honesty and humility, show me a leader who doesn't have both and I'll show you someone the majority of today's enlightened employees don't want to work for.

Don't Be Afraid to Give Someone Else the Credit

What do we need with accolades, anyway? We hand out our own raises, don't we? Nobody gives us performance reviews, and we don't have a boss to impress, and anyway, we motivate ourselves. (If we didn't, we wouldn't be entrepreneurs.)

So give the credit away. Heap it on someone who can put it to work. On a deserving employee perhaps—someone who will devour it, digest it, and multiply it far beyond its original value.

And if, for some befuddling reason, we think those accolades are meant for us, we'd better sign up for an ego test. While there's nothing wrong with a healthy ego in our line of work, it's important that ours be manageable. As well as nurtured from within.

Those that require outside feeding are dangerous.

THE BOTTOM LINE

These aren't management issues, they're leadership issues.

Leadership goes miles beyond management, and once achieved, provides leverage far beyond what management can.

43

What Happens Today Was Yesterday's Fault

Have you ever noticed that the hottest month of the year is August even though the sun is at its peak in June?

And have you ever noticed that the hottest time of the day is midafternoon even though the sun is directly overhead at twelve o'clock?

And have you noticed that your kid never cleans up his room on the same day you ask?

I know there are scientific explanations for the first two situations and I suspect there is a behavioral explanation for the third (something to do with genetics, I'd bet). But whatever the explanations, these lags in time are a reality of life. We must learn how to live with them.

Well, this time lag has a place in our small-business world as well. Here's how it works:

- When our sales hit the skids it isn't because our salespeople have suddenly become lazy. They suddenly became lazy six months ago. The results have just caught up.
- When our days-in-receivables suddenly double, it isn't because

our credit manager went on an extended vacation this week. It's because he went on an extended vacation three months ago.

• When our inventory soars out of sight, it isn't because of what we ordered this month. It was our prior month's purchases that killed us.

And so it is with any bad news. What happens today is yesterday's fault.

Most of the time there are logical explanations for this lag in time. For instance, many years ago I discovered that the sales of the company I was entrepreneuring at the time were always soft in the month of March. It took a while but I eventually determined that the spirit of Christmas was the culprit. That is, our salespeople got swept away in it. They took the month of December off.

And March paid the price.

In addition to holidays, the traumas of life are also high on the list of lag-causing dirty deeds. If our inventory clerk gets married in June, you can bet by the time October comes around our perpetual records will have gone to hell. If our CFO gets divorced in April we can make book that our accounting department will be in the tank by July. If there's a death in the credit manager's family in March, our receivables will be off the charts by September.

Meanwhile, the same thing happens at home. Our kid gets cut from the basketball team in November, and his report card takes the hit in January.

No one is spared. Time gnaws at us all.

So what does this lag in time mean to our small business? It means we must recognize its existence and learn how to compensate for it. Lag is a fact of life and will continue to be until such time as people are replaced by robots.

How do we compensate for it? Maybe we create an incentive for our salespeople (a sales contest, for instance) to get them off their butts in December. Maybe we shore up our inventory handling department (hire a temporary or lend the department a good employee from another unit) before the wedding. Maybe we spend more time with our CFO (manage him carefully, support him tenderly) once we realize his marriage is falling apart.

And one more suggestion on the subject of the negative impact of this time lag. Don't forget, when salary review time comes along, an employee may be setting the world on fire this winter, but he wasn't even smoldering last spring. Reward him for the entire year, not just for the past three months.

The business of business is a twelve-month affair. But people, damn their human souls, have their ups and downs, and so does their performance. It's our job to manage around those ups and down and make sure that the quality of last year's performance coincides with the size of next year's salary increase.

And lest I forget, Christmas and trauma take their toll on entrepreneurs, too. We get no emotional exemptions.

When our art director takes a couple of months off, tomorrow's creative programs go to hell.

When we take a couple of months off, the future of our company goes to hell.

THE BOTTOM LINE

Today's labors are tomorrow's rewards.
Yesterday's letdowns are today's setbacks.

44

The 80-20 Rule

I sold my last company in June of 1990. Stepped into a brand
spanking new career. New disciplines, fresh opportunities, an exciting change in a life that thrives on exciting change.

Not everything in my life changed, however. Some things have
remained constant from one career to the next, like the 80-20 rule
that hovers over my head like an old, familiar hat. For instance,
today:

- 20 percent of my friends give me 80 percent of the friend-
  ship I need.
- 80 percent of my significant output comes from 20 percent
  of my input.
- 20 percent of my writing gives me 80 percent of my
  satisfaction.

And so it goes. The 80-20 rule is hard at work in my new
career.

Just as it was in my last one. Here's how it applied in my small-
business days:

The 80-20 Rule As It Applies to Customers:

- *Eighty percent of my profits came from 20 percent of my customers.*

  What this means to you: Focus your time and your energy on those customers who have the potential to be profitable. Stop wasting your time on those who don't.

The 80-20 Rule As It Applies to Employee Output:

- *Eighty percent of my company's output came from 20 percent of my employees.*

  What this means to you: Intensify your hiring procedures and work harder to improve, or cull, the 80 percent.
      Oh yes, and take damn good care of that 20 percent!

The 80-20 Rule As It Applies to Employee Problems:

- *Eighty percent of my people problems came from 20 percent of my employees.*

  What this means to you: Do something about that 20 percent. Either solve their problems (by training and motivating), or solve your problem. (By training yourself, or upgrading them. Or, as a last resort, culling them.)

The 80-20 Rule As It Applies to the Sales Force:

- *Eighty percent of my sales volume came from 20 percent of my sales force.*

What this means to you: Identify your 80 and 20 percenters. Then take measures to improve, or cull, the 80 percenters.

The 80-20 Rule As It Applies to Expenses:

- *Eighty percent of my P&L waste came in 20 percent of the expense categories.*

What this means to you: While easy money can always be found in the smaller expense categories (the 80 percent), the biggest bucks (and the most sacred ones) are always in the largest categories (the 20 percent).

Begin with the wages and salaries account. Identify the fat, using a zero-base budgeting system, then trim and downsize where necessary.

The 80-20 Rule As It Applies to Excess Inventory:

- *Eighty percent of my excess inventory was in 20 percent of my stock-keeping units.*

What this means to you: Reread the previous 80-20 rule, and follow the same procedures.

The 80-20 Rule As It Applies to Accounts Receivable:

- *Eighty percent of my slow-pay dollars came from 20 percent of my customers.*

What this means to you: Determine the source of that 20 percent; there is usually a common denominator. One salesperson, maybe? One market? One product? Then do something about it.

The 80-20 Rule As It Applies to Headaches:

- *Eighty percent of my headaches came from 20 percent of my responsibilities.*

  What this means to you: Identify the offending 20 percent and do something about them. (Hire someone or train someone or train yourself.)

  Are most of the 20 percent in the financial arena? A new CFO, perhaps? Administrative? A new COO or office manager or secretary? Sales? Operations? Inventory?

The 80-20 Rule As It Applies to Success:

- *Eighty percent of my successes came from 20 percent of my efforts.*

  What this means to you: Find a way to spend more time focusing on whatever it is you're good at, and less on whatever you aren't. Surround yourself with superstars to do the things you don't do well. Or hire a president, or maybe a COO. Learn how to leverage your talents as well as your time.

If this were a perfect world, the 80-20 rule wouldn't be the 80-20 rule anymore. It would be the 50-50 rule.

Imagine how sweet it would be if 50 percent of our sales volume came from 50 percent of our customers. And if 50 percent of our tasks were accomplished by 50 percent of our employees. And if 50 percent of our success came from 50 percent of our efforts.

But alas, this isn't a perfect world. Most of us are doomed to flounder forever in the throes of its 80-20 rule, unless we make a strategic change.

What can we do?

First, set a goal to make it the 75-25 rule.
Then begin chipping away.

THE BOTTOM LINE

The 80-20 rule: it dominates small business, from the output of
its employees to the content of its inventory. Nothing escapes it.
The 80-20 rule is the bane of the entrepreneur. It means too
much time for too few results, in a profession where time is
money, and money, survival.

45

Balance
the Two Sides

I once had a CFO who was twice as intelligent as I. Maybe three times.

That man could count more beans in an hour than I could count in a month. And between counting beans, a constant stream of logic spewed from his mouth, faster than spreadsheet percentages from his Macintosh. Why, this guy had an answer for everything, and what's more, he was usually right. I swear, the left side of his brain had to be the size of a grapefruit.

But despite the fact that his left side was bigger than both of my sides put together, he's destined to be a bean counter forever. That's because his left side overgrew his right side, like a field of smothering crabgrass.

For those of us fuzzy on the nooks and crannies of cranial geography, the left side is where our logic hangs out. You know, the side that adds and subtracts and reads the *New Yorker.* The Mr. Spock side for some folks. The Harpo Marx side for others.

Meanwhile, the right side is the intuitive side, the creative side, the side where our imagination lurks. The side that doesn't make decisions, it makes friends. That side that doesn't make plans, it conjures dreams.

The left side is at its best when counting beans or punching keyboards or playing chess. Doing those things that thrive on reason and logic. But bring unreasonable and illogical people to the party and the right side had better be included on the invitation list.

According to those who study such subjects, the logical left is dominant with most people, and those who fall into this category require a gargantuan effort to swing open the gates to the right side. For those folks I have a suggestion.

Steal a page from sales. Today's successful salespeople have learned to visualize their sales calls before they make them. They conjure a picture of the presentation in advance, including the customer's questions, his possible objections, the asking for the order, and of course, the desired results. This creative process of visualization (which involves opening up the right side) serves three purposes: it creates an agenda, it prepares the salesperson for the unexpected, and it gives him a positive attitude with which to walk in the door.

Well, we nonsales types are capable of visualizing, too. And if we try hard enough, we can visualize ourselves right out of our left side and into the right side.

For instance, try visualizing yourself in an employee's shoes. A production employee, perhaps. Ask what could be done to motivate you to improve whatever it is you do. Then make a list of how you'd respond and conceptualize the results. And before you know it, this dose of visualization, when combined with a shot of imagination, will swing your creative gate open.

And who knows what lurks behind those unopened gates? We'll never find out unless we make the effort to open them.

Once those gates have opened, branch out. Visualize a whole range of opportunities. How can we treat our customers better? How can we cut our expenses? How can we reduce our inventory? How can we upgrade our superstars? Our company is teeming with creative opportunities. Close your eyes. Visualize them.

But remember, it isn't just the right side that makes us a flexible manager. And it isn't just the left side, either. It's the two sides working together, in tandem. It's the balance between logic and creativity that makes for successful management, along with the ability to shift from one side to the other without grinding gears.

My CFO needed a crowbar to open the door to his right side. I needed a doorstop to keep mine shut.

THE BOTTOM LINE

The higher up in management we go, the more the right side of our brain needs to be involved.

The left-siders may have the answers and the right-siders may have the ideas, but it's those who balance the two sides who get the results.

IX

Is the Entrepreneur in the Company's Future?

46

Growth and the Entrepreneur

We've dissected our employees and the role of flexible management in the preceding forty-five chapters; now let's take a few pages to talk about growth and the entrepreneur. (Show me an entrepreneur who doesn't worship growth and I'll show you an impostor. Like glucose and white corpuscles, it's in our blood.)

After all, growth is the American way. And the capitalistic way. And the only way, because American capitalism offers its participants only two options where business is concerned. We either grow or we die, there's no in-between. (Staying the same—stagnation—is not an option. Instead, it's a one-way ticket to Chapter 11.)

But just because growth is necessary to our survival doesn't mean it comes naturally. Or that it's efficient. Or fun.

Au contraire.

For growth always means more hassles, more problems, and more sleepless nights. And the "bigger" our company grows, the more complicated those hassles and problems and sleepless nights become, until someday—and I can guarantee this will happen—we'll wish we were back to square one. Starting up all over again.

Ah, those wonderful words. Start and up. Start-up. We can never recapture the excitement and enjoyment of our first start-up, no matter how hard we try. There's so much energy, so much commitment, so much shared purpose in those early days. No amount of today's bull's-eye management will ever duplicate those founding feelings.

But the euphoria of those early days will pass, you can make book on it. And sooner or later the downsides of growth will rise up and attempt to bury us all. I can't say exactly when that time will come. It will depend on the strength of our niche, the condition of our balance sheet, the industry we're in, our competition, and a host of uncontrollable and random events. And most of all, it will depend on us and our ability to adapt to the pace of our company's growth.

I should know. The downsides of my company's growth consumed me. Five consecutive years of 30 percent sales growth stretched my management skills (along with my company's balance sheet) to their stressed-out limits. The culmination wasn't fatal for the business; it survived to be passed on to new owners. But it was fatal for me. I had burned out—well before my time.

Why must we entrepreneurs, and the businesses we create, suffer so much from the throes of relentless growth?

The reasons are twofold. First, most of us aren't prepared for the managerial demands of that growth. Not only are we unskilled and untrained, but we also don't have the slightest idea how to resolve our escalating problems. And Lord, can they escalate quickly. A company enjoying a 25 percent increase in sales growth will suffer a 25 percent increase in the number of related problems, along with a 25 percent increase in the complexity of those problems. Unless we improve our managerial skills at a corresponding rate, those entrepreneurial skills that got us that far will no longer suffice.

And our company will outgrow us.

Second, the bigger our company becomes the further we fade from the center of the action. Our visions get blurred as a result of that growth and distance. Our dreams fade. Our energy dissipates. The enthusiasm of the start-up becomes little more than a memory.

It's an entrepreneurial axiom that with distance comes misunderstanding. And misdirection. Even lethargy sometimes, because we can't be everywhere at once and the resulting diffusion leads to confusion.

You've heard it before and you'll hear it again—*one-million-dollar small businesses aren't in the same universe with twenty-five-million-dollar emerging companies.* No, make that the same galaxy. The more we grow, the more layers there are to separate us from our customers and our vendors and our employees. Compound this separation with the complexities of rapid growth and it's like Gerald Ford when he inherited the reins from Richard Nixon. The job will be bigger than the man.

No longer will our muscle and adrenaline and enthusiasm sustain our company's growth. Now we must shift to such things as leadership and focus and delegation to get the job done. (And don't forget accountability and communication and training, ad infinitum.) Advanced managerial skills, every one. Foreign to many of us.

Does this mean, then, that we should attempt to downshift our company's growth?

No, but it does mean we had better control that growth, by making the necessary adjustments to keep pace. Adjustments such as planning for tomorrow, and training our employees, and making the necessary changes to existing systems and cultures. Oh yes, and making the necessary changes in ourselves.

So what's all the fuss about? What's the big deal, anyway? What is it that makes it so difficult for us free-spirited entrepreneurs to make this transition from entrepreneur to manager? What makes it so difficult to keep up with our company's growth? To make the necessary adjustments to become a flexible manager?

Funny you should ask. Let me count the ways. . . .

THE BOTTOM LINE

Growth can be dangerous, even fatal, when the entrepreneur doesn't grow as fast as, or faster than, his company.

Planning, training, and sometimes replacing (of systems, employees, and the entrepreneur) are imperative if he is to survive his company's growth.

47

The Enemy Is Us

I'm the first to admit that stereotyping can be dangerous.

Having said that, here we go with some good, old-fashioned stereotyping. Following is a list of entrepreneurial traits that make it difficult (and often impossible) for many of us to make the transition to manager, flexible or otherwise.

How many of the following traits belong to you?

Attention to detail: Who wants to be bothered with details when there are so many important things to be done? Don't worry, we assure ourselves, we'll get back to those details later.

Sure we will. When pigs fly.

Focus: We're the happiest when our plates are the fullest, as we race from project to project with nary a backward glance. The bigger the crisis the better, and we rarely have time to put out one fire before we're fighting the next.

Oh yes, and besides being easily sidetracked, our focus is highly selective. Give us a new sales program, a marketing idea, or a new product and you'll have our undivided attention. Give us a new paper flow system, a five-year quality program, or an innovative health plan and you'll have to excuse us, we have a phone call to make.

Follow-up: As a result of our preoccupation with the crises that always seem to surround us, we're too busy to follow up. Besides, why should we? People should do the job right the first time, shouldn't they? After all, we do.

Conflict: Hey, we have a system for dealing with conflict. When it rears its ugly head, we avoid it. We grit our teeth, shrug our shoulders, and keep our mouth shut. And *poof*, before you can mumble the words Caspar Milquetoast, the conflict disappears.
Temporarily anyway.

Get outa my way: Nobody can do the job better, or faster, than we can. Sure, we could teach, train, and delegate, but we don't have the time. Anyway, our employees can't do the job half as well as we can, and by the time we've finished teaching, training, and delegating, we could've finished the job ourselves. Twice.

Downsides: Why worry about downsides when we don't plan on having any? No siree, not us. Our ink will always be black, our interest rates will always stay low, and the dark clouds of business will forever hover on someone else's horizon. Never on ours.
Downsides are for lawyers and accountants, not for entrepreneurs.

Motivation: Who has the time for all those mind games that managers must play? They're all a waste of time and energy. Not to mention downright unnecessary.
Most people are like us, motivated by the need to create and to grow. So leave them alone; motivation will take care of itself.

Accountability: Damn right people should be accountable! But to whom? And for what?

Organization charts? Job descriptions? Goal setting? Performance reviews? Give us a break. We have better things to do with our time.

Communication: Who needs meetings and memos and endless discussions? Who needs newsletters and manuals and never-ending regulations?

Not us. Just give us a crowbar and a place to stand and we can move the world.

Size: We are as our sales define us. One million in sales, we nod proudly. Or ten. Or twenty-five. Bigger is always better. More is always merrier. That's the entrepreneur's way.

Why not profitability instead of sales? Or return on sales? Or return on assets?

It's that kind of better that is truly better. That's the manager's way.

And so it goes. If we've been your basic textbook entrepreneur, many of the above traits belong to us. They're the reason we selected this lonely career in the first place. And anyway, many of these same traits were directly responsible for our early successes.

But the minute we hire our first employee we need to begin the change, to sublimate our stereotypes. For as sure as our company needs a new breed of management to survive, so many of our old entrepreneurial traits will begin working against us.

And too late we learn that details can kill. And that projects must be completed, and that we can't do everything ourselves, and that profits, not sales, drive growth. And most of all we learn that our employees are *not* like us.

Well, I've got good and bad news for the transitional entrepreneurs among us. The good news is, if we want our employees to pursue our vision badly enough, it can happen.

The bad news? We've got to change. To see the light. The light that comes from realizing that what got us here is no longer enough. If profitable growth is to be our goal, then it's time for the flexible manager in us to emerge.

Unless, of course, our company would be better off without us. A frightening thought, wouldn't you agree?

THE BOTTOM LINE

It isn't fair. The same traits that make for healthy entrepreneurs also account for unhealthy managers.

48

To Be or
Not to Be?

It's a bigger decision than choosing a spouse. Selecting a career. Buying an American car. It may be the biggest decision we'll ever make.

Do we stay? Or do we leave?

Do we hold on? Or do we sell?

Do we attempt to become the manager our company needs? Or do we move on?

Try this. Make a list of all your traits that work against you as you attempt to make the transition to flexible manager. Call it your managerial defects list. Start with whichever of those traits in the preceding chapter apply, then add those particular to you.

Having an introspection problem? (If so, you've just uncovered Managerial Defect number 1.) Ask your spouse for help. And your employees. And your friends. (Having an ego problem? Aha, Managerial Defect number 2.)

How long is the list? How difficult will these managerial defects be to change? How many can be overcome by hiring? By training? By delegating?

How many *must* we change? How many *can* we change? How many do we *want* to change?

I made my list of managerial defects two years before I sold my last company. The list was long—nine major-league entries—ranging from attention to detail (short) to conflict avoidance (ample), with a generous portion of focus and attention span shortcomings stashed in between.

For two years I tried to make the necessary changes. Two long, exasperating, unhappy years they were, too, and ultimately they ended in my failure to make the transition. My managerial defects had proved too major, too numerous, and too deeply ingrained to change. In the process I wasted two years of my life (Lord, I'd love to have them back) and impeded my company's progress as well.

In retrospect, I should have hired a president. (We were $15 million in sales at the time. And profitable, too.) I could have assumed the role of CEO and, after twenty-two years of hard-core entrepreneuring, would have had everything I've ever wanted.

What happened instead? I burned out.

The good news from my attempt? Assuming that Barry Manilow is right ("We learn more from failure than we do from success"), I am one of the world's foremost experts on what it takes to make the transition from entrepreneur to manager.

So here it is, friends. Short and sweet. A list of questions you should ask yourself, if you haven't already:

1. How long is your managerial defect list? How many of the traits on the list can you change? How many can you hire around? Train around? Delegate around?

2. Should you hire a president instead of trying to make the transition yourself? Is your company big enough to warrant one? Profitable enough? Could you let go?

3. Or should you sell? Move on to another start-up? Another career? Something you're better suited for? (And, lest I forget, is your company really salable?)

4. Or should you make a personal commitment to begin a

strategic change—a personal commitment to become a flexible manager?

A word from the wise here. Don't wait until circumstances force you to make these decisions. Make them now.

While you still have time.

THE BOTTOM LINE

Growth necessitates change.
Not minor change. Major change.
Less of the old. More of the new.
Not harder. Smarter.

X

Tips to Grow By

49

The Only Thing
That Is Better
Is Better

"How big is your company?" she asks.

"Ten million," he replies proudly. "And yours?"

"Twenty million," she beams.

She wins.

For bigger, you see, is better. It's the American way.

But is bigger the right way? Why must our measuring stick always be mass of sales? Why not quality of earnings? Depth of equity? Return on sales? Return on equity?

Why in the name of quality must we focus on sales to the exclusion of everything else?

This relentless infatuation with size is a roadblock to our entrepreneurial survival, unless we're drafting defensive tackles or building interstate highways. For bigger is not always better in the business of conducting business. Bigger is only better when certain other, more important criteria have been met. Criteria such as:

- The quality of the team. Read this book again if you haven't ingested this one.

- The state of technology, including systems and controls.
- The strength of the balance sheet. It had better remain ahead of sales growth.

And just as we're hung up on the mass of sales, so we're similarly mesmerized by the rate of sales growth. Not earnings growth, mind you, but sales growth. The company with the fastest sales growth wins, never mind the bottom line. Never mind the soaring debt-to-equity ratio. Never mind the flock of creditors in the background, hovering above us like Ralph Nader circling General Motors.

Any CFO worth his salt can, by juggling a few key numbers, determine the sales growth our balance sheet can afford as a function of our earnings stream. The results of this exercise will tell us, for instance, that assuming earnings of X we can support sales growth of Y. Any more than Y will push key balance-sheet ratios beyond their safety zone. From this exercise we can learn to manage our sales growth to fit the limits of our balance sheet.

And what happens when we stumble beyond the safety zone that orderly growth provides? When we suddenly run short of cash or our inventory balloons to unprecedented heights or our earnings turn blood red?

Why, we attack, of course, and we work harder at whatever it is we do best, which is usually creating more sales.

Well, I've got bad news for those of you who respond in that manner. You've just thrown gasoline on the campfire. And damned if the flames won't reach for the sky, and your hole is about to be dug another notch deeper.

For bigger, you see, is not necessarily better. It only means our exposure grows bigger, that is, unless our earnings grow correspondingly bigger, too.

And more is not always better. It only means our headaches grow bigger, unless our resources grow bigger, too.

In the final analysis, the only thing that is better . . . is better.

THE BOTTOM LINE

Size should be dictated by the quality of employees, the state of technology, and the strength of the balance sheet.

Focus on the means, not on the end. The end will take care of itself.

50

The Rule of
Many Reasons

"The 49ers win because of Montana," I've heard people say.

Or, "The Yankees lose because of Steinbrenner."

Or, "IBM's on top because of its R&D."

So what happens? Montana gets traded, and the Forty-Niners win anyway. And George gets the boot, and the Yankees lose anyway. And IBM spends zillions on R&D, and it only adds to their losses.

Once more the adage is proved. There isn't only one reason why football, baseball, or corporate teams win. Or why they lose. There are many reasons.

If you think it's only the quarterback who wins football games, try playing the game without an offensive tackle. They'll carry the poor QB off the field in the opening minutes. Or give your defensive free safety the Sunday off. Or block shoddily, or tackle meekly, or have each player scarf down a half gallon of ice cream before the game. Just watch, you'll see. There are a myriad of reasons why teams lose.

And if your business is successful, there are a myriad of reasons why your team has won. You've hired right, and fired right, and focused, and made a good product, and put the right distribution system in place, and planned, and strategized, and it goes on forever, the things you've done right.

And if your business has taken a plunge, there are equally as many reasons why. You've hired poorly, or haven't fired when you should, or your quality is poor, or your sales force needs training, or your culture lacks accountability or . . .

That's how the Rule of Many Reasons works. And it applies to everything we do, whether it's running our company or raising our kids or shuffling along the backroads of life.

So what does the Rule of Many Reasons mean to the entrepreneur?

It means there is no easy fix. There are priorities, for sure, but our company won't do a one-eighty tomorrow simply because we've cranked up a quality program. Or started hiring better. Or care about our customers more. Or whatever it is we've started to do that we weren't doing before.

And it means that the winner in the small-business game is the flexible manager who has learned that it's everything that makes the difference. The big things and the little things and the in-between things. Not just sales. Or production. Or the paper flow system. Or efficient meetings. Or clean restrooms. Or the Yellow Pages ads.

It means everything.

And further, this Rule of Many Reasons means prioritizing. And never being satisfied. And paying attention to detail.

Like I said, the Rule of Many Reasons means something of everything. Big and small. New and old.

And it never stops applying. Which is not to say we must make all those reasons happen ourselves. But if we don't, somebody else had damn well better. And it's our job to see that somebody else does, and then it's up to us to make that somebody else accountable. And motivate him, and compensate him and . . .

See what I mean? We're back where we started again.

THE BOTTOM LINE

I Success isn't just one thing. It's everything.   I

51

All We Can Do
Is the Best We
Can Do

I don't know what you've learned from reading this book, but I know what I learned from writing it. Or, I should say, I know what I reaffirmed from writing it.

I reaffirmed that:

1. people are everything to a small business; and
2. the entrepreneur is at the top of the people pile.

Sooooo . . . if we're Wizards of Oz and if it's the levers we pull that determine the success or failure of our company, then it's important, no, make that imperative, that we pull the right levers, not the wrong ones. And for us to pull the right ones, we've got to be thinking straight when we pull them. As in logical. As in the right frame of mind.

But too often we aren't logical or in the right frame of mind. That's because there are too many entrepreneurial depressants tugging at our emotions. Depressants such as:

▪ Responsibility to our employees. At one time, two hundred employees depended upon me for their paychecks. That's four hundred mouths to feed and, brother, that's pressure.

- The never-ending, overhanging cloud of debt. My bank line once topped $7 million, which was ten times my net worth at the time. Every penny (gulp) guaranteed by me.
- The fear of failure. The lingering specter of Chapter 7, the entrepreneur's own, personal version of the grim reaper.
- Responsibility to our family. Entrepreneurial failure doesn't mean just losing a job. It means losing everything.

Put these four depressants together and what do you have? The opportunity for vast quantities of frustration, self-doubt, and guilt.

Show me an entrepreneur who hasn't felt frustration, self-doubt, and guilt and I'll show you an entrepreneur who is new to the game. And show me an entrepreneur who hasn't shaken off that frustration, self-doubt, and guilt, and I'll show you an entrepreneur who is perched somewhere on the sidelines. Permanently.

Those who survive this career of ours will be those who come to terms with themselves. Those who learn we can't do it all. Those who learn that "all we can do is the best we can do."

"All we can do" means all we can learn, and all we can try, and all we can give of ourselves. Anything less isn't all we can do.

And "the best we can do" comes from all we can do. Once we've done the best we can do, there's nothing left to be done.

So lighten up, my friend, you've made it this far. You've defied the odds, which is more than can be said for the majority of those folks who have entered this career.

THE BOTTOM LINE

I If you've done the best that you can, what more is there to do? I

52

My Top Ten Tips

A review of my top ten tips, for the current or aspiring entrepreneur:

1. Don't Make the Same Mistakes
Your Predecessors Made.

Fight loneliness with all the energy you can muster. Either:

- Find a partner with complementary skills or
- Find a mentor or
- Use an outside board of directors (or board of advisers) or
- Read everything you can get your hands on or
- Join small-business and trade associations or
- Take advantage of U.S. government offerings or
- All of the above

2. Every Company Has Four or Five Game-breaking Positions. The Entrepreneur's Number One Responsibility Is to Assure These Positions Are Filled with Superstars.

These game-breaking positions include the CFO, along with the operations, sales, marketing, and purchasing managers. And, oh yes, you. The entrepreneur. Your job is to hire the right people, train them, reward them, and make sure they grow as fast as or faster than the company's sales.

And if they don't keep up, your job is to replace them. For their sake as well as your own.

3. The Best Employees Go to Those Who Are Willing to Go to the Most Trouble to Find Them.

Hiring the best employees makes the entrepreneur's life easier. The good ones don't require motivating or baby-sitting, they only need training and liberating.

4. Nothing Happens Until a Sale Is Made.

How many good products go nowhere because they don't reach the shelves?

It's sales and distribution that drive the business. Develop a sales-and-customer-driven culture.

5. Fast, Good, and Cheap. Pick Any Two.

You can't be all things to your customers. Don't even try.

My advice? Pick fast and good. Leave the cheap to someone else.

6. All Turnarounds Require a Strategic Change.

Never try to grow your company out of its problems. More sales only mean more headaches.

Strategic change means new missions, new directions, and often, new players (sometimes including the entrepreneur).

Smarter, not harder.

7. The Entrepreneur's Resources Are Finite. Focus on What You Can Achieve.

It is better to solve one problem forever than to have three in various stages of irresolution.

8. Learn to Live in Today's Environment. Things Never Go Back the Way They Were.

Quality, service, expense controls, employee benefits, interest rates, information processing, communications. Everything is in a state of continual change.

Forget the past. Celebrate change. Things will never go back the way they were.

9. Acknowledge Your Mistakes.

Nobody is right all the time. It's OK for your employees to make mistakes, as long as they don't make the same one twice.

And it's OK for you to make mistakes, too. But fess up. You aren't fooling anyone.

10. Vendors Are Partners, Too.

Good vendors are as important as good customers.

Treat them as partners, not as adversaries.

Index